Mishkat Al Anwar

The Niche for Lights

Imam Ghazali

Translated by W.H.T Gairdner

Dar Ul Thaqafah

Dar Ul Thaqafah
www.darulthaqafah.com
https://twitter.com/darulthaqafah
Email: darulthaqafah@gmail.com

Find our titles on your favourite online bookstore using the keyword 'Dar Ul Thaqafah'

AUTHOR'S PREFACE

I am so conscious that my general equipment was insufficient to warrant my having undertaken an *introduction* to this treatise (in addition to the translation), that my utmost hope is this,—that what I have written may be regarded by lenient Orientalists as something to elicit—provoke, if you will—the necessary supplementing and formative criticism ; or as useful materials to be built into some more authoritative and better-informed work : and that they may from this point of view be inclined to pardon what otherwise might seem an unwarrantable piece of rashness and indiscretion.

A still greater presumption remains to be forgiven, but this time on the ground of the great human simplicities, when I venture to inscribe this work, in spite of everything, to the beloved memory of

Ignaz Goldziher

—that golden-hearted man—who in 1911 introduced me to the Mishkāt ; and to join with his name that of

Duncan Black Macdonald,

who first introduced me to the Mishkāt's author. Of these twain, the latter may perhaps forgive the lapses of a pupil because of the filial joy with which, I know well, he will see the two names joined together, howsoever or by whomsoever it was done. As for the former, . . . in Abraham's bosom all things are forgiven.

Cairo.
July, 1923.

ACKNOWLEDGMENT

I HAVE greatly profited from hints, generously lavished in the course of correspondence, from Professors D. B. MACDONALD, R. NICHOLSON, and LOUIS MASSIGNON, in addition to recent works by the last two. My cordial thanks to these; and also to Professor D. S. MARGOLIOUTH for discussing with me some of the difficult points in the translation.

CONTENTS

[Ghazzālī's sections and titles have been supplemented. The page-references enclosed within square brackets in the Introduction, Translation, and foot-notes are references to the pages of the Arabic text,[1] the numbers of which will be found in the text of the Translation, enclosed in square brackets.]

TRANSLATOR'S INTRODUCTION

TRANSLATION OF MISHKĀT AL-ANWĀR
"THE NICHE FOR LIGHTS"

PART I. LIGHT, AND LIGHTS: Preliminary Studies.

PART II. THE SCIENCE OF SYMBOLISM.

---

[1] Cairo, A.H. 1322; Maṭbaʿat aṣ Ṣidq.

INTRODUCTION

[The references in square brackets are to the pages of the Cairo Arabic edition, and to the present English translation.]

THE MISHKĀT AL-ANWĀR[1] is a work of extreme interest from the viewpoint of al-Ghazzālī's[2] inner life and esoteric thought. The glimpses it gives of that life and thought are remarkably, perhaps uniquely, intimate. It begins where his autobiographical *Al-Munqidh min al-Dalāl* leaves off. Its esotericism excited the curiosity and even the suspicion of Muslim thinkers from the first, and we have deeply interesting allusions to it in Ibn Ṭufail[3] and Ibn Rushd,[4] the celebrated philosophers of Western Islam, who flourished within the century after al-Ghazzālī's death in 1111 (A.H. 505)—a fact which, again, increases its importance and interest for us.

I. DATE, OBJECT, AND GENERAL CONTENTS

There is no way of fixing the precise date of this treatise ; but it falls among his later ones, perhaps among the latest ; the most important hint we get from Ghazzālī himself being that the book was written after his *magnum opus*, the *Ihyā' al-'Ulūm* (p. [9]). Other works of Ghazzālī mentioned by him in this treatise are the *Mī'ār al-'Ilm*, *Maḥakk al-Naẓar*, and *al-Maqṣad al-Asnā*.

The object of the opuscule is to expound a certain Koran verse and a certain Tradition. The former is the celebrated Light-Verse (S. 24, 35) and the latter the Veils-Tradition. It is divided into three sections, of which the first is considerably the longest.

In this first section he considers the word " light " itself, and its plural " lights ", as applied to physical light and lights ;

---

[1] The *Mishkāt al-Anwār* is numbered No. 34 in Brockelmann's *Geschichte der Arabischen Literatur* (vol. i, p. 423). It was printed in Cairo (maṭba'at aṣ Ṣidq, A.H. 1322), to which edition the references in the present work are made. There is another edition in a collection of five opuscules of Ghazzālī under the title of the first of the five, *Faiṣal al-Tafriqa*.

[2] The Algazal of the Schoolmen.

[3] The Abubacer of the Schoolmen.

[4] The Averroes of the Schoolmen.

to the eye ; to the intelligence (i.e. intellect or reason) ; to prophets ; to supernal beings ; and finally to Allah himself, who is shown to be not the only source of light and of these lights, but also the only real actual light in all existence.

In the second section we have some most interesting prolegomena to the whole subject of symbolic language in the Koran and Traditions, and its interpretation. Symbols are shown to be no mere metaphors. There is a real mystical nexus between symbol and symbolized, type and antitype, outer and inner. The symbols are infinitely numerous, very much more numerous than those mentioned in Koran or Traditions. *Every* object on earth " perhaps " has its correlative in the unseen, spiritual world. This doctrine of symbols reminds us of the Platonic " ideas " and their earthly copies, and of the " patterns of things in the heavens " and " the example and shadow [on earth] of heavenly things " in the Epistle to the Hebrews. A notable deduction is made from this doctrine, namely, the equal incumbency of keeping the outward letter (*ẓāhir*) of the Law as well as its inner meaning (*bāṭin*). Nearly all the most advanced Ṣūfīs were zealous and minutely scrupulous keepers of the ritual, ceremonial, and other prescriptions of the Sunna law, and Ghazzālī here supplies a quasi-philosophical basis for this fidelity—a fidelity which some of the bolder and more extreme mystics found illogical and " unspiritual ".

In the third section the results of this symbolology are applied to the Verse and Tradition in question. In the former the beautiful, and undeniably intriguing, expressions of the Koran—the Light, the Niche, the Glass, the Oil, the Tree, the East and the West—are explained both on psychological and religio-metaphysical lines ; and a similar exegesis is applied to the tradition of the Seventy Thousand Veils.

II. Mysteries left Veiled in this Treatise

In the course of all this Ghazzālī gives us, incidentally, much that excites our curiosity to the highest degree ; though

always, when we get to the crucial point, we meet a
" perhaps ", or a patronizing allusion to the immaturity of
his less-initiated reader. (Ghazzālī's hesitations—" it may
be," " perhaps," etc.—are worthy of study in this treatise.
They do not so much leave the impression of hesitancy in his
own mind, as of a desire to " fence " a little with his reader.)
He himself writes " incommunicable mystery " across a
number of these passages. Thus, the nature of the human
intelligence and its peculiar affinity to the divine (pp. [6, 7]) ;
the mystic " state " of al-Ḥallāj, and other " inebriates ",
and the expressions they emit in their mystic intoxication
(p. [20])—" behind which truths," says Ghazzālī, " also lie
secrets which it is not lawful to enter upon " ; the astounding
passage (p. [24]) in which to the supreme Adept of the mystical
Union with deity are ascribed features and functions of very
deity ; the real explanation of the word *tawḥīd*, involving as
it does the question of the reality of the universe and the
nature of the soul's union or identification with deity ; the
nature of the Commander (*al-Muṭāʻ*) of the universe, and
whether he be Allāh or an ineffable supreme Vicegerent ; who
that Vicegerent is, and why it must be *he* and *not* Allah who
performs the prime function of the cosmos-ruler, viz. the
issue of the command for the moving of the *primum mobile*,
whereby all the motions of the Heavenly (and the Sub-
lunary) spheres are set a-going ; and the final mystery
of Allah-*an-sich*, a Noumenal Deity, in whose case transcendence is to be carried to such a pitch that gnosticism
and agnosticism meet, and the validity of every possible or
conceivable predication is denied, whether of act or attribute
(see p. [55])—all these things are incommunicable mysteries,
secrets, from the revealing of which our author turns away at
the exact moment when we expect the *dénouement*. The art
is supreme—but something more than tantalizing. Who were
the adepts to whom he *did* communicate these thrilling secrets ?
Were these communications ever written down for or by his
brother initiates ? Or did he ever communicate them ?
Was there really anything to communicate ? If so, what ?

III. A GHAZZĀLIAN PHILOSOPHY OF RELIGION

On the whole it is the final section on the Veils Tradition which, though really of the nature of an appendix, contains the most numerous and the most interesting problems for the study of Ghazzālī's inner life, thought, and convictions. This tradition speaks of " Seventy Thousand Veils of Light and Darkness " which veil pure Godhead from the human soul. The origin of the tradition is, it is safe to hazard, Neoplatonic, and it therefore lent itself completely to the gnostic and theosophical mode of thought which so soon invaded Muslim Ṣūfism, after its less successful effort to capture orthodox Christianity. Accordingly Muslim mystics seem to have seized upon the tradition with avidity, though they interpret it variously. For an entirely Neoplatonic, theosophical interpretation, as expounded by Rifā'ī dervishes, the translator's " ' Way ' of a Mohammedan Mystic " may be consulted.[1] According to this version, the soul, in its upward Seven-fold Way to Union with pure Deity, is at every stage stripped of 10,000 of these Veils, the dark ones first and then the bright. After that the naked soul stands face to face with naked Deity, with Absolute Being, with an unveiled Sun, with unadulterated Light. Ghazzālī's treatment is different. According to him, these Veils are various according to the varieties of the natures which they veil from the One Real. And it is the classification of these natures, which is thus involved, that supplies rich material for an unusually *inside* view of Ghazzālī's real views concerning men, doctrines, religions, and sects. It is not the orthodox schoolman, the fierce dogmatist, the rigid *mutakallim*, who is now speaking. We have the sensation of overhearing Ghazzālī as he speaks aloud to his own soul, or to a circle of initiates. It is hardly less than an outline of a philosophy of religion with which we have to do. He divides mankind into four classes : those veiled with veils of pure darkness ; those veiled with

---

[1] *The Moslem World*, year 1912, pp. 171 seqq., 245 seqq. ; as separatum, Otto Harrassowitz, pp. 9, 10.

veils of mixed darkness and light ; those veiled with veils of pure light ; and those who attain to the vision of the Unveiled. Every line of this part of the work merits and requires the closest study. It is not possible to give this detailed study here—it has been given elsewhere, and to that the reader must be referred.[1] But a summary of Ghazzālī's classification of souls and creeds may be given here, for thus, even more effectively than by an extended study, may a vivid preliminary appreciation be gained of the importance of this section for students of the Ghazzālī problem. He begins at the bottom and works up the light-ladder, rung by rung, to the very top, thus giving a gradation of human natures and human creeds in respect of their approach to absolute truth. Sometimes the grades are definitely identified by the author. In other cases they may be certainly, or nearly certainly, identified from the description he gives. In the following summary Ghazzālī's *own* identifications are given between round brackets ; *inferred* identifications, certain or nearly certain, between square brackets.

Class I.—Those veiled with Veils of pure Darkness
Atheists—(*a*) Naturist philosophers whose god is Nature,
      (*b*) Egotists whose god is Self.
Subdivisions of (*b*) :—

(1) Seekers after sensual pleasures (the *bestial* attributes).
(2)   dominion
     ("Arabs, some Kurds, and very
     numerous Fools ")   (the *ferocious*
(3) Seekers after filthy lucre   attributes).
(4)   vainglory

Class II.—Those veiled with Veils of mixed Darkness and Light
A. THOSE WHOSE DARKNESS ORIGINATES IN THE SENSES

(1) Image-worshippers.
    [Polytheists of the Hellenic (? and Indian) type.]

[1] *Der Islām*, year 1914, in Nos. 2 and 3 ; by the present writer.

6   AL-GHAZZALI'S MISHKAT AL-ANWAR

(2) Worshippers of animate objects of physical beauty.
(Some of the most remote Turkish tribes.)

(3) Fire-worshippers.
[Magians.]

(4) Astrologizing Star-worshippers.
[Star-worshippers of Ḥarrān : ? Ṣābīans.]

(5) Sun-worshippers.

(6) Light-worshippers, with their dualistic acknowledgment
of a supreme correlative Darkness.
(Zoroastrians of the cult of Ormuzd and Ahrimān.)

B.   THOSE WHOSE DARKNESS ORIGINATES IN THE IMAGINATION
(φαντασία)

(who worship a One Being, sitting [spatially] on his throne).

(1) Corporealists.
[Extreme Ḥanbalites : Zahirites.]

(2) Karrāmites.

(3) Those who have eliminated all spatial ideas in regard
to Allah except the literal " up-above ".
[Ibn Ḥanbal.[1] Ḥanbalites.[2]]

C.   THOSE WHOSE DARKNESS ORIGINATES IN THE [DISCURSIVE] [3]
INTELLIGENCE

[Various sorts of *Mutakallimīn*]

(1) Anthropomorphists in respect of the Seven Attributes
of Allāh, " Hearing, Seeing," etc., and especially
the " Word " of Allāh.
(Those who said that the Word of Allāh has letters
and   sounds   like   ours.)   [Early   literalists :
Ḥanbalites : early Ash'arites.]

---

[1] *Faiṣal al-Tafriqa*, p. 10.

[2] Averroes adds to these (with justice) the Koran ; Mohammed himself ; the " Early Fathers " ; al-Ash'ari ; and the early Ash'arites
" before the time of Abul Ma'ālī ", says Averroes, loc. cit., i.e. of
al-Juwainī, the Imām al-Ḥaramain, our author's Shaikh, d. 478 (see his
al-Kashf 'an manāhij al-adillā', ed. Müller, p. 65, Cairo ed., p. 54).

[3] For according to Ghazzālī the genuine axiomata of the pure intelligence
are infallible. See p. [10], and an important autobiographical passage
near the beginning of the *Munqidh.*

(2) Those who said that the word of Allāh is like our mental speech (*hadīth al-nafs*).
[Later Ash'arites.]

Class III.—Those veiled by pure Light
[i.e. purged of all anthropomorphism (*tashbīh*)]

(1) Those whose views about the Attributes were sound, but who refused to define Allāh by means of them : replying to the question " What is the Lord of the Worlds ? " by saying, " The Lord, who transcends the ideas of these attributes ; He, the Mover and Orderer of the Heavens."
[Ḥasan al-Baṣrī, al-Shāfi'ī, and others of the *bilā kaifa* school.]

(2) Those who mounted higher than the preceding, in declaring that Allāh is the mover of only the *primum mobile* (the Ninth and outermost Heaven), which causes the movement of the other Eight, mediated by their respective Angels.
[Ṣūfī philosophers. (?) Al Fārābī.]

(3) Those who mount higher than these again, in putting a supreme Angel in place of Allāh, Who now moves the heavens by *commanding* this supreme Angel, but not immediately by direct action.
[Ṣūfī philosophers. Al-Ghazzālī himself when *coram populo* (*Munqidh*, p. 11) !]

Class IV.—The Unveiled, who Attain

Those who will predicate *nothing whatsoever* of Allah, and refuse to allow that He even issues the order for the moving of the *primum mobile*. This Commander (*Muṭā'*) is now a Vicegerent, who is related to the Absolute Being as the sun to Essential Light or live coal to the Element of Fire.

(1) Adepts who preserve self-consciousness in their absorption in this Absolute, all else being effaced.

      (2) Adepts whose self-consciousness is *also* effaced (" the
               Fewest of the Few ") [al-Hallāj and the extreme
               Mystics],
         (*a*) who attain to this State with a single leap—
            as Abraham " al-Khalīl " did,
        (*b*) who attain to it by stages,—as Mohammed
            " al-Ḥabīb " did [at the *Mi'rāj*].

IV. Ghazzālī Problems Raised by the Foregoing

The mere perusal of this graded scale of systems and of souls
shows at once its extraordinary interest because of its revelation of Ghazzālī's innermost thought about these things; and
because of the piquancy and difficulty of some of the problems
raised. In the discussion of the whole subject the reader is
referred to the monograph upon the *Mishkāt* to which allusion
has been made. The problems may be indicated here in the
form of questions, for the sake of defining them as particularly
as possible : —

(1) How is it that some reputable Moslems are grouped
with Idolators and Dualists in the second division (" mixed
light and dark ") ?

(2) How is it that Jews and Christians are neither mentioned
nor alluded to in this rather full sketch for a philosophy of
religion ? And where could they have been fitted in if they
had been mentioned ?

(3) How is it that the later Ash'arites, the standard orthodox
Theologians, are placed so low, viz. in the division where
there are still veils *of darkness* ?

(4) How is it that the Mu'tazilites are neither mentioned nor
alluded to ; and that, according to the differentia of the
highest section of the second division, it would be inevitable
to place them *above* the orthodox Ash'arites ?

(5) How is it that the most pious believers of the earliest
and most venerated type come no higher than the *lowest*
section of the third division ?

(6) How is it that to such men is ascribed *any* special concern about Allāh *as " mover of the Heavens "* [1] ?

(7) How is it that the various doctrines about the mode of this Moving of the Heavens is made the main if not the sole differentia of the (*ascending*) grades of this division, though in other works Ghazzālī treats this very matter with marked coolness [2] ? How is it that on *this* is explicitly said to turn the superiority of the schools of Ṣūfī's over the pious Believers, and the superiority of one school of Ṣūfī's over another ?

(8) How is it that this matter of Moving the Heavens is considered so particularly to threaten the Unity of Allāh, and that that Unity is only saved when He is relieved from even the function of Commanding the (outermost) Heaven to be moved ?

(9) *And who is this Commander who thus commands, and who orders all things, and who is related to pure Being as the Sun to Elemental Light ?* And what was " the mystery (in this affair), the disclosure of which this book does not admit of " ?

(10) What becomes of a Deity of whom nothing whatsoever can even be said or predicated ? And how, then, can a " relation " between Him and His Vicegerent be asserted, still more described as above ? And how can this Unknowable, Unimaginable, and Inconceivable be nevertheless " reached " by mystic souls ?

(11) What was " the book " into which Ghazzālī himself says he put all his esoteric teaching (*Jawāhir*, p. 31) ; which he implores any into whose hands it may fall not to publish ; which Ibn Ṭufail denies could have been this *Mishkāt* (*Ḥayy*, ed. Gautier, pp. 13–15, trans. Gautier, pp. 12–14), nor any other of the supposed esoteric books that " had come to Andalus " ?

---

[1] This is all the more marked because the words italicized are Ghazzālī's own gloss on a quotation from the Koran ; see below.

[2] e.g. *Tahāfut*, pp. 57, 60.

V. The Problem of the Vicegerent in Ibn Rushd and Ibn Ṭufail

After this it will cause no surprise that it is this figure of the Vicegerent (*al-Muṭā'* . . . *alladhī amara bi taḥrīk il-samāwāt*) who excited the curiosity and suspicion of thinkers in the century after Ghazzālī's death. The passage is at least twice singled out, once by Ibn Rushd in the treatise already cited, and once by Ibn Ṭufail in his *Ḥayy ibn Yaqẓān*.

(1) Ibn Rushd uses the passage to level at Ghazzālī a direct accusation of gravest hypocritical insincerity over a matter which Ghazzālī had ostentatiously singled out as the prime test of orthodoxy, namely, the doctrine of *emanation*. According to Ibn Rushd the passage about the Vicegerent was the explicit teaching of this doctrine of the Philosophers, for which, elsewhere, Ghazzālī can find no words strong enough to express his censure and contempt. The words of Ibn Rushd are as follows :—

" Then he comes on with his book known as *Mishkāt al-Anwār*, and mentions therein all the grades of the Knowers of Allah ; and says that all of them are veiled save those who believe that Allah is not the mover of the First Heaven, *He being the One from Whom this mover of the First Heaven emanated* : which is an open declaration on his part of the tenet of the philosophers' schools in the science of theology ; though he has said in several places that their science of theology (as distinct from their other sciences) is a set of conjectures." [1]

It is not within the scope of this Introduction to follow in detail the evidence for and against the truth of this radical accusation. This has been done at length and with considerable minuteness in the monograph in *Der Islām*, which has already been cited (pp. 133–145). The reader must be referred to that ; and it must suffice here to say that after the full consideration of all the evidence the verdict given

---

[1] Op. cit., ed. Müller, p. 21, Cairo edition, p. 59. The treatise was written before A.H. 575 ; date of *Mishkāt c.* 500.

there is Not Guilty. On the other hand, the existence of an
esoteric doctrine in regard to this Vicegerent and his function
is undeniable (and undenied) ; and it is clear, from the comparison of the *Mishkāt* itself with the *Munqidh*, that that
doctrine differed vitally from the one professed by Ghazzālī
exoterically (*Munqidh*, p. 11). Ghazzālī himself, in a passage
of remarkable candour,[1] admits that every " Perfect " man
has three sets of opinions (*madhāhib*), (a) those of his own
environment, (b) those he teaches to inquirers according as
they are able to receive them, and (c) those which he believes
in secret between himself and Allāh, and never mentions
except to an inner circle of friends or students.

Ibn Rushd's accusation was an attempt to identify the
figure of the Vicegerent, *al-Muṭā'*, with that of *Al Ma'lūl
al Awwal*, the First Caused, in the emanational scheme of the
Neoplatonizing[2] philosophers of Islam, with al-Fārābī and
Ibn Sīnā at their head. This was the Demiurge, the Being
who first emanates from the Absolute Being, and mediates
between It and all the lower stages of relational existence,
with their increasing limitedness and grossness, thus relieving
the predicateless Absolute from all part in the creation *or
administration* of the universe.

There can be no doubt that whatever Ghazzālī's doctrine
of the Vicegerent was, and whatever else his esoteric doctrine
contained, the emanational theory formed no part of that
doctrine. For this particular piece of pseudo-metaphysics he
appears to have had a very particular dislike and contempt ;
and if Ibn Rushd was really serious in levelling his accusation
he can hardly be acquitted of being blinded by his bitter
prejudice against " Abu Ḥāmid ". The only possible ground
for Ibn Rushd's accusation which I have been able to dis-

---

[1] *Mīzān al 'Amal*, p. 214.

[2] The unquestionable Neoplatonism of much of the forms and expressions
of Ghazzālī's thought, if not of the thought itself (see especially pp. [15,
16, 29, 47 seq.]), exposed him in a very special way to this charge of emanational pantheism. And it cannot have made it easier for him to steer clear
of such dangers in fact.

cover is as follows :—it is a fact that the extreme (*ghulāt*) Imāmites did identify *al-Rūḥ* " The Spirit of Allah " with the First Emanation.[1] If, as is contended hereafter, Ghazzālī identified *al-Muṭā‘* with *al-Rūḥ*, and Ibn Rushd was aware of this, he may have thought, or been pleased to think, that Ghazzālī therefore thought that *al-Muṭā‘* was the First Emanation. This would be an indirect confirmation of the identification which it is attempted presently to prove, namely, *al-Muṭā‘* = *al-Rūḥ*.

(2) We now pass to the other criticism of the passage, by Ibn Rushd's contemporary Ibn Ṭufail, in the introduction to his philosophical romance entitled *Ḥayy ibn Yaqẓān*.[2]

Ibn Ṭufail's allusion to this perplexing passage is as follows :

" Some later writers [3] have fancied they have found something tremendous in that passage of his that occurs at the end of *al-Mishkāt*, which (they think) impales Ghazzālī on a dilemma from which there is no escape. I mean where, after speaking of the various degrees of the Light-Veiled, and then going on to speak of the true Attainers, he tells us that these Attainers have discovered that this Existing One possesses an attribute which negates unmitigated Unity ; insisting that it necessarily follows from this that Ghazzālī believed that the Absolute Being has within His Essence some sort of plurality : which God forbid ! "

The excursus on this passage in the article cited from *Der Islām* (pp. 145–151) can only be summarized here. It seems to have escaped the critics quoted by Ibn Ṭufail, that the Unveiled, according to Ghazzālī himself, *abandoned* the position of the last of the Light-Veiled just because of this dread, viz. that the identification of *al-Muṭā‘* with Allāh would endanger " the unmitigated Unity " of Deity. Ibn

---

[1] Massignon, *Hallāj*, p. 661.

[2] Ed. Gautier, pp. 13–15, transl. 12–14.

[3] Or " a later writer ", presumably Ibn Rushd himself, in the passage already cited and discussed.

Ṭufail himself, though he admits the serious contradictions which appear in Ghazzālī's books, flatly refuses to see in this passage anything so monstrous, or anything sinister at all.

Unfortunately he does not give us his own exegesis of the passage ; but it may perhaps be inferred from his own schematization of the grades of being. In this he makes elaborate use of the schema of reflectors, and reflectors of reflectors, which Ghazzālī has already suggested in this book (pp. [15, 16]). " The essences of the Intelligences of the Spheres " are represented as successive, graded reflections of the Divine Essence. The highest of them " is not the essence of the One Real nor is he the Sphere itself, nor is he other than them both. He is, as it were, the image of the sun which appears in a polished mirror ; for that image is neither the sun, nor the mirror, nor other than them both ". It is probable that Ibn Ṭufail, who professed to have won through to his position after studying al-Ghazzālī and Ibn Sīnā (the juxtaposition is singular !), would have more or less equated this conception of the highest Essence of the Intelligences of the Spheres with the conception of *al-Muṭā‘* in the *Mishkāt*, though he says nothing about the business of Heaven-moving in relation to this Being. It need not follow that al-Ghazzālī would have accepted this explanation [1] ; though both men were evidently striving equally to avoid a total pantheism, and both disbelieved in the emanational theory as taught by al-Fārābī and Ibn Sīnā.

VI. One Solution of the Problem of the Vicegerent

In the absence of " the book " into which Ghazzālī put these secret opinions, or inconceivable mysteries, including, we may suppose, the secret of this mysterious Vicegerent, we are not likely to reach any authoritative settlement of the question : nor, even if we be put on the right track, to clear up the whole of the mystery. For want of direct help from

---

[1] Though his " mirror " schema in *Mishkāt*, p. [15], is near Ibn Ṭufail's meaning.

our author, therefore, the only thing to be done is to examine minutely *al-Mishkāt* itself, to see if it yields any indirect help. It would seem that from this examination two possible solutions emerge. In this section the first of these will be discussed.

This solution, which was first suggested to the writer by the distinguished French Orientalist, M. Louis Massignon, identifies the mysterious figure of this Vicegerent, *al-Muṭā'*, with the *Quṭb* (" Axis ") or some other Supreme Adept. According to the developed doctrine, this *Quṭb* was an earthly Mystic of supremest attainment, who during his lifetime administered the affairs of the heavens and the earth. There was nothing about him, during his lifetime, to suggest to any observer that he was engaged in so stupendous a task, and it was not known till after his death that he had been " the Axis of his time " (*quṭbu zamānihi*).

The beginnings of this doctrine go back far beyond al-Ghazzālī—a rudimentary form of it was held by even the ultra-orthodox Ḥanbalites,[1] and a developed form of the conception is expressed quite definitely in al-Hujwīrī's *Kashf al-Maḥjūb*,[2] and must have been widely held, in orthodox circles too, in the fifth century, at the close of which our treatise was written.

Moreover, at least from the time of al-Ḥallāj, to whom, as we shall see, our author in this treatise refers in terms by no means of repudiation, the very word under discussion, *al-Muṭā'*, or some other form of the same verb, occurs in significant connexion with supreme sainthood. One of the accusations levelled against al-Ḥallāj was that he taught that " having attained to sainthood the Adept becomes *al-Muṭā'*, he who says to a thing ' Be ! ' and it becomes ".[3] It sounds startling enough, but it was a true accusation, though it has to be taken in connexion with the whole of Ḥallāj's

---

[1] Massignon, *Passion d' al-Ḥallāj*, p. 754.

[2] p. 214 of trans.

[3] Massignon, op. cit., 791 ; ib., p. 472.

philosophy of mystical union with the Divine.[1] For he did definitely adopt from a predecessor, Ibn ʿIyāḍ, the aphorism " *Man aṭāʿa Allaha aṭāʿahu kullu shay'* ",[2] an aphorism which received a later redaction (quite in the spirit of Ḥallāj, as has been shown), " *man hudhdhiba . . . fa yaṣīru muṭāʿan, yaqūlu lish shay'i ʿ Kun ʾ fa yakūn*," " He who has passed through the mystic askēsis becomes Obeyed ; he says to this or that, ʿ Be ! ʾ and it is." [3]

Since then al-Ḥallāj did so teach, and did use this very word, and since al-Ghazzālī in this treatise betrays a very considerable admiration of al-Hallāj, and a sort of tremulous half-assent to his wildest utterances, including the notorious " *Ana-l Ḥaqq* " itself, it would seem that a strong prima-facie case has been made out for identifying the *Muṭāʿ* of our treatise, in spite of the cosmic nature of his functions, with some supreme Adept. But only a prima-facie case. To make out the thesis itself, the treatise itself must be interrogated ; for it by no means follows that because a Ḥallāj held an opinion a Ghazzālī adopted it.

There are, certainly, some passages that do suggest that the solution is along this line.

(1) The description of the adventures of a soul in highest state of Union (*Mish.*, p. [24]) tends to bear out the identification, or the general idea underlying it. The person there described is a supreme Adept, and in particular al-Hallāj himself. Having reached Union with the One divine Real, he ascends in and with Him " to the throne of the Divine Unity and from thenceforth administers the Command throughout His (or ʿ his ʾ, for in this extraordinary passage the pronouns remain the same throughout) storied Heavens ". The words translated " administers the Command ", *yudabbiru-l*

---

[1] The sense in which he *did* use the expression, and the proof that it did not in his thought mean self-deification, is given very clearly in Massignon, op. cit., pp. 519–521.

[2] Op. cit., p. 472.

[3] *al-ʿAynī on al-Istakhrī ;* quoted in a letter by M. Massignon to the writer.

amr, are remarkable, for they contain an Arabic word (*amr*) which, as we shall see presently, is to the last degree significant, being the very word used in the *Muṭā'* passage (p. [55]), where Ghazzāli confesses it is an obscure mystery. The *Muṭā'* (Commander) is said to move the outermost Heaven by precisely this *amr* (command). The words *yudabbiru-l amr* could no doubt be translated in a less significant way, owing to the troublesome double meaning of *amr* (" affair," " command "), namely, " he disposes things." But in view of the fact that this *amr* was a notable Ṣūfī term, and a mysterious problem alluded to by Ghazzāli in this very treatise, it seems inevitable to take it as " command " here. And a " Command " necessitates an " Obeyed ".

(2) On p. [23], where the reference throughout is purely general, and presumably applies to *anyone* who has the necessary qualifications and attains to this supreme mystical " state ", Ghazzāli says that when the mystic Ascent is complete, " if there be indeed any change, it is by way of ' the Descent into the Lowest Heaven ', the radiation from above downwards." This also suggests supreme divine activity in the Universe below, especially if the word *ishrāq* refers, as it probably does, to causative activity.

(3) On pp. [13, 14] occurs another passage which strongly supports the general identification, though it leaves its particular and personal reference still obscure. In this the adepts, who in their mystical Ascent (*mi'rāj*) " attained to that supreme attainment ", are said to be " *the Prophets* ", who " from thence looked down upon the entire World Invisible [precisely the world of the Heavens] : for he who is in the world of the Realm Supernal is with Allāh, *and hath the keys of the Unseen*. I mean that *from where he is descend the causes of existing things* ; for the world of sense *is one of the effects of yonder world of cause* ", etc. This looks almost like a reasoned, philosophic doctrine behind the mystical one, that to Attain to the world of Reality is *ipso facto* to attain to the fount of causation ; which involves the ability to direct

the Causes which control all the Effects in the Heavens below and the Earth beneath. The Vicegerent does no more than this.

A close scrutiny of these passages leaves one, nevertheless, with the impression that the Adepts whose celestial adventures are there described are too generalized, or perhaps one should say too pluralized, to be identifiable with this single, solitary figure of *al-Muṭā'* as he is presented in our passage. As far as these three passages go, this assumption of the reins of the Universe is only granted to Adepts in their mystic " States ", to Prophets in their highly exceptional " Ascents ". There is nothing to show that two or more such Attainers might not exist at one time, or that even one must always be existing ; in other words, there is no trace of the *complete* and fully developed *Quṭb* doctrine in this treatise. But these considerations make it impossible to identify any one of these Adepts, or all of them together, with the cosmic *Muṭā'*, whose function, related as it is to the very mechanism of the Heavens, is ceaseless, and coextensive with Time itself. And these last four words suggest a further consideration which in itself seems fatal to the proposed identification ; namely, that *al-Muṭā'* was Vicegerent *from the very foundation of the world* ; he is the one " who commanded the Heavens to be moved " (p. [55, 1. 12]). No Ḥallāj, no Adept, no *Quṭb*, no Prophet even, ever claimed, or had claimed for him, such priority as this,[1] or even priority at all. But if not, none of them—and, if so, no terrestrial being at all—can claim to fill the rôle of this Vicegerent. The three passages were probably intended only to assert and account for the *karāmāt* of the Saints in their wonder-working, which was parallel to that of the Koranic Jesus.

The a-priori question of our author's attitude to the *Quṭb* doctrine—whether, consistently with his published writings, he *could* have sustained such a doctrine in this work—is one

---

[1] The question of the priority claimed by a certain school for *Mohammed*, and of the *nūr Muḥammadī*, will be considered later.

which can only be indicated here.   Professors R. Nicholson
and D. B. Macdonald have both communicated to the writer,
in reference to the passage under discussion, their opinion
that there is an a-priori *im*possibility.   To al-Ghazzālī the
doctrine was tainted with Imāmism, his special *bête noire*
(see his attack on the Ta'līmites in his *Munqidh*) ;[1] that since
an omnipotent Administrator must also be an infallible Guide
(whom Ghazzālī would not have at any price), there is no room
for the former in Ghazzālī's thought (thus Professor
Macdonald).   If the *Muṭā'* is not Mohammed, he is certainly
no Saint (thus Professor Nicholson).

Be this as it may, the above considerations, drawn from
the study of the text itself, and from the passages which
prima-facie seemed to point to the *Quṭb-Muṭā'* identification,
seem finally, when more closely examined, to rule that
identification out.

VII.   ANOTHER SOLUTION

But there are other passages in our treatise which, when
carefully studied, lead to the belief that in Ghazzālī's own
mind—though the identification is nowhere explicitly stated
or even significantly hinted at—the *Muṭā'* is none other than
al-Rūḥ, THE SPIRIT OF ALLĀH.[2]

In S. 17, 87, Mohammed himself had left this enigmatic
entity as a divinely uncommunicated, and therefore incommunicable, mystery.   The passage runs as follows :
" They ask thee of The Spirit : say, The Spirit pertains *to my
Lord's Word-of-Command*, and ye have not been communicated
knowledge [of It] save a little."   The Arabic of the words
italicized is *min amri rabbī* ;   and we are again faced, at the
outset, with the troublesome double meaning of the word *amr*.
The phrase *min amr* might merely mean—perhaps *did*

---

[1] See Nicholson, *The Idea of Personality in Ṣūfism*, p. 46.

[2] Ibid., pp. 44, 45.   The identification had occurred independently to
the present writer before the appearance of Professor Nicholson's work.
It had also occurred independently to Professor D. B. Macdonald.

only mean—"a *matter* of"[1] (my Lord's), a vague phrase, common in Arabic, meaning "something that pertains to" so-and-so. But in a case like this, we are not concerned with what Mohammed may originally have meant, but what mystic writers have taken him to mean. And enormously though this verse attracted, puzzled, and baffled commentators and mystics of all ages, the latter seem to have taken the word *amr*, with practical unanimity, in the far more significant sense of "Command". The Hebrew root means "speak", and this meaning is implicit in the Arabic root also, which signifies *spoken* command. And just as later Jewish writers made out of a derivative of this root a Logos doctrine (*Memra*), so the Mohammedan mystics came near to making a Logos doctrine out of the word *amr*, taking their start from this very text.

A mystery having been definitely started by this text, a haze of mystification was thrown over the entire subject of "spirit": over angels as "spirits", over the human "spirit", the prophetic "spirit"; the inter-relation between these, and the relation of all to "the Spirit"; finally *Its* relation to Allāh. In our treatise there is a full measure of this mystification.

"The Spirit" is *ar-Rūh*. With this may be absolutely identified *Rūh Allāh* "The Spirit of God"; *Rūhuhu* "His Spirit"; and *al Rūhu-l Qudus*[2] (or *Rūhu-l Qudsi*) "The Transcendent Spirit"—all Koranic expressions.

What then are the considerations which suggest that we have in this Figure of Mystery the key to the mystery of the Vicegerent? On this supposition there would be no wonder that Ghazzālī left the figure of the latter a mystery, and

---

[1] The word *min* is itself tantalizingly ambiguous. It might mean "(derived) from" or "(part) of" or "pertaining to". Under such circumstances one looks round for the vaguest possible phrase to render the preposition.

[2] This is the Arabic for the Christian "The Holy Spirit". But in Arabic as in early Hebrew the word emphasized the idea of separation or transcendence rather than of righteousness or holiness.

declined to divulge the secret of it (p. [55]). He *could* not divulge the whole secret, because by the decree of Allāh and the Book, he could not know it himself—" save a little." And there is no wonder he declined to discuss it, considering the interminable complexities and baffling obscurities of the recorded musings of Ṣūfī doctors on the theme.

At the very outset we are struck by the fact that the word *Muṭā'* occurs in the Koran (S. 81, 23), and not only so, but it occurs as an attribute of the mysterious Agent of Revelation, the vision of whom Mohammed saw at the first (S. 53, 5–16). The text 87, 23, is not definitely cited in *Mishkāt*; and in later Islam the commentators, with their arid tameness, made a stereotyped identification of this Figure with the Angel Gabriel. But the Koran gives no warrant for this; and there is nothing in the *Mishkāt* to show that Ghazzālī thus taught. On the contrary, Gabriel is assigned a low place in the angelic hierarchy.[1] No one can read those two Koranic passages (in S. 87 and S. 53) without feeling that Mohammed's awful Visitant *on those two occasions* was the One of absolute supreme rank in the heavenlies : not *a* spirit but *the* Spirit. And It was *muṭā'*—" one who is obeyed." Is it not but a very short step from this to *al-Muṭā'*, *The* Obeyed-One ?

The identification, however attractive, would nevertheless be precarious if there was not so much in the *Mishkāt* itself that supports this identification.

(1) On p. [15] the ultimate kindling-place of the graded Lights, of which the Prophets occupy the lower and terrestrial ranks and the Angelic Beings the higher and celestial, is the theme of discussion. Both these ranks of beings are compared to " *lights* " and *all* of them are contrasted with the Highest of all, who is compared to " *fire* ", from whose flame these graded lights are successively lit, from top to bottom. Who and what is this Highest of all, next to Allāh ? He is said to be " ' an Angel with countenances seventy thousand '. . . . This is he who is contrasted with all the angelic host, in the

<hr>

[1] M., p. [16].

words : '*On that day whereon* THE SPIRIT *ariseth, and the Angels, rank on rank.*' " It is thus explicitly clear that this Being is the highest of all possible beings in heaven or earth next to Allāh; and so, if the Vicegerent of p. [55] is *also* the highest of all, it would seem inevitable to equate them.

(2) In the very next page, p. [16], Ghazzālī schematizes this conception, and, comparing Allah with the *Sun* (the source of light in the terrestrial system), he compares the highest of the ministrant lights to the *Moon* (all others being reflections, or reflections-of-reflections, of *it*). This " Highest is the one who is nearest to the Ultimate Light : . . . that Nighest to Allāh, he whose rank comes nighest to the Presence Dominical, which is the Fountain-head of all these Lights ". This " Nighest " and " Highest " cannot be other than THE SPIRIT spoken of in the preceding page. And on p. [31]—unless Ghazzālī has suddenly changed all the symbols—the Sun is said to be the Sovereign, while " the antitype of the Moon will be that Sovereign's *Minister* (*wakīl*), for it is through the moon that the sun sheds his light on the world in its own absence, and even so it is through his own *wakīl* that the Sovereign makes his influence felt by subjects who never beheld the royal person ". Does not this *wakīl* who stands " highest and nighest " to his Liege-Lord, and who makes himself obeyed by all that Lord's subjects, strongly suggest " the Obeyed One ", *al-Muṭā‘*, the Vicegerent of the conclusion, whose function is, precisely, this ?

(3) But what perhaps clinches the matter is the tell-tale word *amr* in that passage about *al-Muṭā‘* himself on p. [55]. Those who stopped short of complete illumination, he says, identified *al-Muṭā‘* with Allāh just *because* he moves the *primum mobile* (and so all things) " with his Word of Command " (*amr*). " The explication of which *amr* (he continues), and what it really is, contains much that is obscure, and too difficult for most minds, besides going beyond the scope of this book." And then he says that the *perfect* Illuminati perceived that *al-Muṭā‘*, the Obeyed One, is not more than

the Highest-other-than-Absolute-Deity, and is related to Him as the sun to Essential Light (mysterious enough this !) or as a glowing coal to the Elemental Fire : and therefore they turned their faces from that Being " who commanded (*amara*) the moving of the Heavens " to the One Existent, Transcendent, Incomparable, Predicateless.

With this word *amr* thus impressed on us with such penetrating significance we turn back to the Koran text : " The *Spirit* pertains to my Lord's *Word of Command* (*amr*) . . ." Unless the word *min* introduces a quite upsetting element, the identification between this SPIRIT and the Commander who is Obeyed seems complete.

But the history of the Ṣūfī teaching on the text shows that *min* need introduce no such upsetting element, and that the practical identification of *Amr* with *Rūḥ*, of The Word of Command with The Spirit, was with the Mystics a familiar idea. It was the explicit teaching of al-Ḥallāj[1] ; and the typical " word of command " which this Divine Spirit gave was the fiat " *Kun!* " " Be!".[2] We have seen the fascination which this treatise shows al-Ḥallāj had for al-Ghazzālī. Does it not seem likely, nay almost certain, that in his meditations on this inscrutable text he followed al-Ḥallāj in this equation, with whatever mental reserve regarding the Spirit itself—whether divine or creaturely, eternal or originate? Not that it was only Imāmites or extreme Ṣūfī Sunnites like al-Ḥallāj who asserted the divinity of The Spirit. The ultra-orthodox Ḥanbalites " admitted in some manner the eternity of the *Rūḥ Allāh* ".[3] Ibn Ḥanbal himself had given them the lead with a characteristic hedging aphorism (which reminds us of similar remarks on the *Ṣifāt*, the *Kalām Allāh*, and the

---

[1] Massignon, op. cit., pp. 519–21.

[2] This mediation of the creative function would carry with it the mediation of the administrative. In this connexion use would unquestionably be made of S. 7, 53, " the sun, the moon, and the stars are compelled-to-work by His *amr* "—His Word-of-Command > His Spirit—exactly the function of *al-Muṭā'*.

[3] Massignon, op. cit., p. 664.

Qur'ān), " Whoever says that *al-Rūḥ* is created (*makhlūq*) is a heretic : whoever says that It is eternal (*qadīm*) is an infidel." [1]   His followers held fast on to " *uncreate* ", and it was hard to keep " *eternal* " from following. No wonder al-Ghazzālī gave a unique and mysterious tinge to his similitude for " The Obeyed ", and that It figures, virtually, as an Arian Logos. The more one reflects on what is said about the function of this Being in M., p. [55], and especially Its comparison with the Sun (Allāh being Essential Light), or with glowing coal (Allāh being Elemental Fire), the more unique It appears, and the more mysterious our author's thought about It becomes. For *such* functions, and *such* a relation to Absolute Deity, are in very truth entirely unique, in kind as well as degree ; and, thus described, the Vicegerent becomes, in a secondary way, as unique a Figure as is Deity Itself. No wonder the passage raised doubts as to the soundness of our author's monotheism ! No wonder he was not anxious to go more deeply into the matter, out of consideration for the limited spiritual capacities of his readers ! Perhaps, to preserve his own faith in the Unity, Indivisibility, and absolute Uniqueness of Allāh, he was glad to leave the dark problem of the Vicegerent where Allāh Himself had left that of the Spirit—an uncommunicated and incommunicable mystery, which now he only knew in part, and only saw as in a glass, darkly.

It remains to consider whether there is any evidence that Ghazzālī extended the equation *Muṭā'* $=$ *Amr* $=$ *Rūḥ* to include the *Nūr Muḥammadī* (as suggested tentatively by Professor R. Nicholson in his lectures on " The Idea of Personality in Sūfism " [2]), the archetypal spirit of Mohammed, the Heavenly Man created in the image of God, and regarded as a Cosmic Power on whom depends the order and preservation of the universe. If this could be sustained it would

[1] Ib., 661.
[2] pp. 46, 47, and Lecture III.

to some extent modify the conclusion reached before that *al-Mutā'* had nothing to do with any human being, idealized or not, whether a Prophet or even Mohammed ; though even so, there would be a vast difference between this archetypal Spirit and the historical Prophet.

While the germs of this idea, as of every other one, may be found much earlier than Ghazzālī's century (the fifth), the study of the sketch which M. Massignon gives of the history of the doctrine (*Hallāj*, pp. 830 seqq.) does not create the impression that it was developed or received in orthodox circles [1] up to Ghazzālī's time. Professor Nicholson does not find it in an orthodox Ṣūfī writer earlier than 'Abdu-l Qādir al-Jīlānī (b. 471, d. 561), in the generation immediately succeeding that of Ghazzālī.[2] After which the doctrine developed and spread amazingly, reaching its height with Ibn al-'Arabī al-Jīlī several centuries later.[3]

Thus the a-priori evidence is this time decidedly against Ghazzālī's having anything to do with this doctrine. Unless, therefore, very clear actual evidence were found in his writings, it would be surely justifiable to assert definitely that it is not Ghazzālian. It appears *not* to be found in his works other than *al-Mishkāt*. If this is so, it may be further asserted with confidence that it is not found in *al-Mishkāt* either. On the contrary, there is much there that shows a relatively simple, primeval conception of Mohammed on the part of Ghazzālī. For him the archetypal man is Adam, as in the Koran, not Mohammed.[4] An examination of the passage [5] in which the idea of the " Khalīfa " appears shows that here also his thought was not esoteric, and that Mohammed was not in his mind : he is thinking of the whole human race, or of Adam himself, the first and representative human being, the

---

[1] It was at first prevalently Imāmite and Shī'ite (Nicholson, *Idea of Personality in Ṣūfism*, p. 58).

[2] He described Muḥammad as *al-rūḥ al-qudus* and *rūḥ jasad al-wujūd* " the Transcendent Spirit, the Spirit of the body of the Universe ".

[3] Nicholson, op. cit., p. 59.

[4] M., p. [34].   [5] M., p. [22].

only " Khalīfa " particularized by the Koran. And the one
passage in the *Mishkāt* which at first sight does look as if
it contained a " high doctrine of the person " of Mohammed,
turns out on closer inspection to prove the exact reverse,
viz. that essentially he belonged to this world and to the
time-order—to the prophets, *above* whom are ranked the
celestial " Lights " culminating, as we have seen, in the
Supreme Angelical, The Spirit. This passage is on pp. [14, 15].
Here we have the Transcendent Spirit Prophetical (*al-Rūḥ
al-qudus al-nabawī*) attributed to Mohammed as prophet,
by reason of which he is called a Luminous Lamp (*sirāj
munīr*). If this stood by itself we might be suspicious of
something esoteric. But immediately after this the other
prophets, and even saints, are said to be " Lamps ", and to
possess, as Its name implies, this Spirit Prophetical. The
sequel shows that this Spirit is the Fire from which all the
Angelical lights above and the Prophetical lights beneath are
lit, and that this Spirit is the Supreme Angelical, " The Spirit,"
as in the passage already discussed.[1]

To sum up the conclusion to which I have been led by a
consideration of the evidence of the *Mishkāt* itself, together
with the a-priori evidence which supplements it and is checked
by it,—the heavenly Vicegerent is the Spirit of Allāh, the
Transcendent Spirit of Prophecy, the divine Word-of-Command ; he is not a *Quṭb* or any Adept ; he is not Mohammed
nor the archetypal spirit of Mohammed.

Whether this mystery of the Vicegerent was connected in
our author's mind with that of the divine-human, archetypal
Ṣūra, as developed by al-Ḥallāj and other advanced Mystics,
will be discussed later.

---

[1] See above, pp. 20, 21. The only thing that puzzles is that Ghazzālī
sometimes distributes and pluralizes this Spirit, see p. [15, l. 4], and p. [22,
l. 8]. In each case the regulative singular, however, is close by. This
reminds one of Rev. iv, 5 and v, 6, compared with Rev. ii, 7.

VIII. AL-GHAZZĀLĪ AND THE SEVEN SPHERES

The Seven Planetary Heavens played a great part in Platonic,[1] Neoplatonic, and Gnostic-theosophical schemes. The naive adoption by Mohammed (in the Koran) of the Ptolemaic celestial construction was one of the things which added picturesqueness to early Mohammedan tradition and theology; caused endless trouble to generations of later theologians; made it easier for Neoplatonic ideas to graft themselves on to Islam; gave to the raptures of the Mystics sensuous form and greater definition; and afforded to the Philosophers a line of defence, and even of attack, in their war with the Theologians.[2] And the allusions of the Koran were heavily reinforced by the legend of the *Mi'rāj*, the exact origin of which is obscure, but which appears in a highly developed form almost from the first. The influence of the pictures and symbols of the *Mi'rāj* are indeed evident in page after page of the *Mishkāt*.

Al-Ghazzālī's sympathies in regard to this subject were divided. He disliked the Philosophers, and this made him displeased with their confident assertions about the Heavens, while he detested the " philosophical " profit to which they put them. On the other hand, he was a Ṣūfī, and thus in closest touch with persons who made very similar assertions about the Heavens, and also put them to profit in their own way. Finally, he was an 'Asharite Theologian, belonging to a school which had recently, after much trouble, eliminated from theology the dangerous ideas to which Mohammed's naive attitude to the Heavens had given rise.

 This uncertainty of touch comes out, as might be expected, in a treatise like *al-Mishkāt* with its blend of scholasticism and Neoplatonically-tinctured mysticism. The Heavens figure continually in its pages. They seem to play a most important part both in thought and in experience—towards the close

---

[1] See the *Vision of Er in the Republic*, bk. x.
[2] See Averroes' *Kitāb al Kashf an manāhij al adillā*, quoted above on p. 6, note 2.

of the book a *determining* part. Yet it is impossible to make
out exactly what that part was, in the mind of Al-Ghazzālī
himself.

On p. [23] we have a correlation of the human micro-
cosm and the macrocosm of the celestial realm, Ptolemaically
construed, in describing the Ascension of a God-united soul.
The adept's body-and-soul structure is conceived of as sub-
sisting in three planes or Spheres, which are correlated with
the three lower spheres of the Seven Planetary Heavens.
From the highest of these (the Intelligence) the soul takes
its departure and ascends through the four upper Heavens
(*ila saba'i ṭabaqāt*) to the Throne [beyond the outermost
Heaven]. Thus he " fills all things " by his upward Ascent
just as Allāh did by His downward Descent (*nuzūl*).
In all this the pronoun " he " stands for the soul *who is now
Allāh-possessed and united*, as described in what immediately
precedes. It is the upward ascent of *Allāh* (corresponding
to His *nuzūl ila-l samā'i-l dunyā*), and not of the Adept
only.

On the other hand, in p. [29], this Ascent is described in
purely psychological terms, without this schema of the
Heavens. And on p. [13] we have the following : " Do not
imagine that I mean by the World Supernal the World of
the [Seven] Heavens, though they are ' above ' in respect
of part of our world of sense-perception. *These* Heavens are
equally present to our apprehension and that of the lower
animals. But a man finds the doors of the Realm Celestial
closed to him, neither does he become of or belonging to that
Realm (*malakūtī*), unless this earth to him ' be changed into
that which is not earth ; and likewise the heavens ; ' [1] . . . and
his ' heaven ' come to be all that transcends his sense. This
is the first Ascension for every Pilgrim who has set out on his
Progress to the nearness of the Presence Dominical." And
he continues : " The Angels . . . are part of the World of

---

[1] S , 14, 48.

the Realm Celestial, floating ever in the Presence of the Transcendence, whence they gaze down upon our world inferior."

The last lines hardly give us the same ultra-spiritualizing impression which is conveyed by their predecessors. And, as we have already seen (Introduction, pp. 7–9), the part played by the Spheres with their Angels in the last section of the book is decisive, and there does not seem to be *there* any spiritualizing whatever.

How far, therefore, these passages are mere word-play, pious picturesqueness, or how far they represent speculation of a rather far-reaching character, is one of the puzzles of the book. In the *Tuhāfut*, in demolishing the arrogant claim of the Philosophers to *prove* their doctrine of the Spheres by syllogistic demonstration (*burhān*), he said : " The secrets of The Kingdom are not to be scanned by means of such fantastic imaginations as these ; Allāh gives none but His Prophets and Saints (*anbiyā'* and *awliyā'*) to scan them, and that by inspiration, not by demonstration." [1] So then there *were* mysteries and secrets in regard to the Spheres. In the *Mishkāt* we are able to see pretty clearly that Ghazzālī had his ; but we are not able to see just what they were. He has kept *this* secret well.

IX. Anthropomorphism and Theomorphism in al-Mishkāt

The doctrine of *mukhālafa*—that the divine essence and characteristics wholly and entirely " differ from " the human —appears to be asserted, as this treatise's *last* word, in its most extreme and intransigent form. For the conclusion of the whole matter, the end of the quest for truth for those who " Arrive ", is " an Existent who transcends ALL that is comprehensible by human Sight or human Insight . . .

---

[1] Tah., p. 60. Quoted in the writer's article in *Der Islām*, see pp. 134–6, 151, 152, where parts of the subject are gone into in greater detail.

transcendent of and separate from every characterization that in the foregoing we have made." [1]

Nevertheless, the *Mishkāt* itself seems to be one long attempt to modify or even negate this its own bankrupt conclusion. Indeed, it goes unusual lengths in asserting a certain ineffable *likeness* between Allāh and man. It is true that the usual anthropomorphic expressions—the Hand, the Session on the Throne, the Descent to the Lowest Sphere, etc., those perennial sources for Mohammedan theologizing—are used and are discounted in the usual way. But they are, in reality, only discounted by being replaced by a Ṣūfī system of theomorphism. This has three main aspects—

(1) a quasi-Platonic doctrine of terrestrial type and celestial antitype ;

(2) the relation of the divine and human *rūḥ* (spirit) ;

(3) the relation of the divine and human *ṣūra* ("image," "form," μορφή).

(1) The whole of the first two parts of the treatise are practically an exposition of an Islamico-Platonic typology. It is not explicitly said that earthly things are more or less faint copies of "the patterns of things in the heavens", though this is probably implicit in what *is* said, namely, that the heavenly realities (*haqā'iq*), ἰδέαι (*ma'ānī*), all have their symbols on earth. These symbols or types, as their Arabic term itself suggests (*amthāl*), do possess a "resemblance" to their celestial antitypes, for, as al-Ghazzālī remarks, "the

---

[1] In Ghazzālī the most extreme Agnosticism and the most extreme Gnosticism meet, and meet at this point ; for, as he says (p. [25]), "things that go beyond one extreme pass over to the extreme opposite." For him "Creed because Incredible " becomes " Gnosis because Agnoston ". What saved the *Universe* for him from his nihilistic theologizing was his ontology (see below, pp. 35 seqq.). What saved *God* for him from his obliterating agnosticism was the experience of the mystic leap, his own personal *mi'rāj*. This may have been non-rational, but it was to him experience. Even those who regard the sensational experiences of Ṣūfism as having been pure self-hypnotism cannot condemn them, and the sense of reality they brought, in relation to the man who had thought his way out of both atheism and pantheism, and yet would have been left at the end of the quest, by his thinking alone, with an Unknown and Unknowable Absolute.

thing compared (*al-mushabbah*, the antitype) is in some sort
parallel, and bears resemblance, to the thing compared
therewith (*al-mushabbah bihi*, the type or symbol), whether
that resemblance be remote or near ; a matter again which
is unfathomably deep." [1]   Ghazzālī can hardly be allowed to
elude the application of this true principle to Allāh Himself,
considering that this very Koran-verse which it is the object of
the entire treatise to expound begins with a simile.   " Light "
is the chosen, or rather the God-given symbol, wherewith Allāh
is " compared ", and which therefore He must " in some sort
resemble ".   This analogy of light floods the whole book.
Now Allāh is the Sun : now the Light of lights : and at the
end, in the same breath in which Abu Ḥāmid, with the
incorrigible inconsistency which so angered Averroes, denied
the validity of all similitude, description, relation, or even
predication in regard to Allāh, we are told that He stands in
relation to His Vicegerent (or " wakeel " in a parallel passage)
as the pure *Light*-essence to the sun, or as the Elemental
Fire to a glowing coal.   Theomorphism has " in some sort "
been admitted.

(2) In the *Iḥyā' al 'Ulūm* Ghazzālī speaks of the human
rūḥ as *amr rabbānī* " a divine affair " (*amr* must surely bear
here its other meaning) ; and he is there very anxious, not to
say agitated, over the esoteric character of the doctrine ; it
must be kept a dead secret from the Many ! it must not
be set forth in a book ! [2]   " The specific characteristic which
differentiates humanity [from the lower creation] is something
which it is not lawful to indite in a book." [3]   The thing that
agitates him is the relation of this human *rūḥ* to the Spirit of
God, *rūḥ Allāh*, and Its relation to Allāh.   The matter is
esoteric—it is to be " grudged " to the " commons "—
because it is dangerous ground. It is dangerous ground because

---

[1] M., p. [14].

[2] See *Mīzān*, p. 214, quoted above.

[3] *Iḥyā*, iv, 294, quoted in a letter to the writer from Professor R.
Nicholson.

one has to walk warily in order to avoid a violation of the uniqueness of Allāh, which would involve confusing Creator with created, and so passing gradually to *ishrāk*, which is the worst " infidelity ".

This particular anxiety is not reflected in the present treatise ; it is strange that the mystery of *rūḥ* does not figure in the list (see above, p. 3) over which the author's *favete linguis* ! is inscribed.[1] He is mainly occupied with working out what the New Testament calls the " operations ", rather than the nature, of the spirit. In so doing the singular " spirit " becomes plural " spirits ", *aruāḥ*, which, as already observed, happens also in the Book of the Revelation. Ghazzālī works out the theory of the several " spirits " of the human psychology ; then the graded " spirits " of the heavenly hosts ; and then the Neoplatonic or theosophic idea of the gradation of all these (in *maqāmāt*), and the way in which they are " lit " (*muqtabasa*) from each other in order : we must not say " derived ", for that would involve him in the emanationism he was ever anathematizing, yet for ever incurring the suspicion of.[2] In all this his tone is open, easy, confident. The special mystery of *The* Spirit had been already discounted in the Koran, so that was harmless. As for the identification of *Rūḥ-Muṭā'*, if our theory is correct, *that* was a grand secret. But that secret he never intended even to hint at, and it would really seem as if we had surprised and betrayed a *sirr maknūn* !

(3) It was the *ṣūra* tradition,[3] "ALLĀH CREATED ADAM AFTER HIS IMAGE," that above all else led Moslem thinkers into temptation—the temptation of trenching on the uniqueness of Allāh. Its very riskiness seems, however, to have fascinated them supremely from the very outset. Not one of them could let it alone. In this very treatise Ghazzālī returns to it again and again. Perhaps it would accord with

---

[1] The human *'aql* does figure on that list, pp. [6, 7].

[2] See the writer's op. cit. in *Der Islām*, pp. 138–141.

[3] Gen. i, 27, though Islām ignores the parentage.

inner truth to say rather that both he and others returned to that tradition not so much as moths fascinated by a dangerous glare, but as those who are feeling cold return for warmth and cheer to even an alien fire. The aphorism, sacred as a Koran text, was the assertion and pledge that man somehow is, or may become, "like God." The word *ṣūra* became the symbol and the guarantee of theomorphism.

In the first allusion in the *Mishkāt* to this tradition (p. [9]), the point of the similarity is the human intelligence (*'aql*). In virtue of his *intelligence*, Ghazzālī hints, man is "after the image of Allāh". The *'aql* is "Allāh's balance-scale upon earth".[1] In its own sphere it is infallible.[2] From the *'aql*, as from a firm "taking-off" place, souls make their mystic Ascension to the heavenlies.[3] It is because it is thus the specifically human faculty that it is a determinative element in the human *ṣūra*.[4]

The second allusion (M., p. [24]) carries us very much further—even to that verge from which Moslem mystics so often looked dizzily down, but from which they so seldom fell, into the pantheistic abyss. Behold a human soul in completest Union (*jam'*) with Deity, sitting on The Throne, and administering all things in heaven and earth ! "Well might one," says our author, "in looking upon such an one," get a new view of this tradition. Is not such a uniate, indeed, "after the image of Allāh" ? But, he continues, "after contemplating that word more deeply one becomes aware that it has an interpretation like [al-Ḥallāj's] 'I am the One Real'."[5] Unfortunately he has omitted to indicate what precisely that interpretation is. We have a tantalizing author to deal with.

What was that interpretation ?

---

[1] M., p. [20].　　[2] Ib., p. [10].　　[3] Ib., p. [24].　　[4] Ib., p. [40].

[5] How translate this " *Ana-l Ḥaqq* " ?　Not by Jesus' " *I am the Truth* ", tempting though this is. "*I am the Absolute*" would be a parallel rendering in modern philosophic parlance. Professor Nicholson's "*I am God*" is startling, but illuminating because perfectly justifiable ; for *al-Ḥaqq* and *Allāh* are mutually and exclusively convertible.

Probably we do not find it in the third passage (pp. [34, 35]), though it is deeply influenced by Ḥallājian thought. There is in the celestial world something which "développe, modalise, et concerte entre elles les créations divines . . . une certaine structure interne particulière à l'acte créateur ".[1] This living order, this organized "Presence" (ḥaḍra), is symbolized by the word *Image*, or *Form*. And this macro-cosmic *ḥaḍra* has its earthly counterpart in an analogous *human* form, or *ṣūra*, which has the same "structure interne particulière " (it is alluded to on p. [22, l. 1], and p. [34, l. 3], and described in detail on pp. [39–41]). Therefore, man, formed in this Form, is " after the Form, the Image, of this Merciful One (*al Raḥmān*) ". Ghazzālī's explanation of his preference for this variation of the text of the tradition, to which, however, he by no means always adheres, is difficult to follow. But the general idea clearly is that " but for this ' mercy ' [i.e. of these two correlative and coincident Forms] every son of Adam would have been powerless to know his Lord, for ' only he who knows himself knows his Lord ' ". The wheel has, indeed, brought us round a strange circle! Through the eternal grace of theomorphism we win back to a higher anthropomorphism, so that the proper study of God is— man! And this from the writer whose last word is that Allāh must not have so much as an attribute predicated of Him, or the divine uniqueness will be violated! Truly, thus the whirligig of thought brings in his revenges.

We have already seen many indications that before he wrote this treatise Ghazzālī must have been deep in the study of al-Ḥallāj; and the passage we have just been considering may be added to these indications. Yet there is no overt trace in it, or elsewhere in the *Mishkāt*, of al-Ḥallāj's profoundest thought on this matter of the Divine-Adamic

---

[1] Massignon, op. cit., p. 519, describing Ḥallāj's doctrine of the divine *rūḥ*, and exactly hitting off Ghazzālī's difficult thought on p. [34, ll. 2, 3] (cf. p. [22, l. 2]). But from this point of view *rūḥ* and *ṣūra* merge into each other, as a careful comparison of the two *Mishkāt* passages just cited shows.

μορφή ; no trace of that strange Figure—that Epiphany of humanized Deity, or Apotheosis of ideal-Humanity—which was presented by Allāh to the angels for worship or ever the first man was created, and in which He Himself, on behalf of the human race, swore unto Himself the Covenant (*mīthāq*) of allegiance. For this conception, which has the closest interrelations with all the moments of the above discussion—*rūh, amr, λόγος, ṣūra, nūr-Muhammadī*—the reader must be referred to the grand work which has brought to light so many hidden things, M. Louis Massignon's *La Passion d' Al Hosayn-ibn-Mansour al-Hallāj*.[1]   Ghazzālī's silence on this so remarkable development of the *Ṣūra* tradition would suggest that it was precisely here that he felt it dangerous to follow al-Hallāj.   What was possible for the seer might send the theologian over the line where Islām ends and pantheism begins.   On the other hand, is it possible that here we have the explanation of our author's embarrassed words on p. [55] "on account of a Mystery which it is not in the competence of this book to reveal"?   His inmost thought may have been, " Perhaps al-Hallāj has penetrated here to something of what the Koran itself [in the Spirit-Verse] left obscure.   I neither assert, nor deny.   *Allāhu a'lam* ! "

Thus we come to the ultimate question—the ultimate question with every Ṣūfī writer and book—does he and it escape pantheism ?   What light comes from this " Niche for Lights " upon this obscure question ?

X.   Pantheism and al-Ghazzālī, in *al-Mishkāt*

The root question in regard to al-Ghazzālī, and every other advanced mystic and adept in Islām, is the question of Pantheism :   did he succeed in balancing himself upon the

---

[1] pp. 485, 599–602.   In a note Massignon hazards the tentative suggestion that this epiphanized God (called by al-Hallāj *al-Nāsūt* in contradistinction from the unknowable *al-Lāhūt*) is analogical to, or suggestive of, Ghazzālī's *Vicegerent* (p. 601, n. 5).   The suggestion is thrilling, as we see.   It must be repeated that there is no overt trace of the doctrine in M-

edge of the pantheistic abyss, and finding some foothold for his creationist theism, some position that cleared his conscience towards his orthodox co-religionists ?   Or did he fail in this ? The *Mishkāt* contains a good deal that is relevant to this final issue.

It contains much, in the first place, which on the face of it reads like naked pantheism ; and in particular the whole passage on pp. [19, 20] and [22–4], where not only is the most extreme language of the extreme wing of Ṣūfism (*Ana-l Ḥaqq* [1] and the rest) quoted with guarded approval, but there is open eulogy of the formula *lā huwa illā Huwa* "there is no it but He", which is declared to be more expressive of real, absolute truth than the Mohammedan creed itself *lā ilāha ill-Allāh* " there is no god but God ".   This would seem to be as unreserved an assertion of flat pantheism as could be found in philosophic Hinduism itself.   Equally worthy of philosophic Hinduism is Ghazzālī's " *He is everything* : He is that He is : none but He has ipseity or heity at all . . . " (p. [22]).   And then again the experience of the advanced Initiates and Adepts is described in terms of thorough pantheism : to them " the plurality of things fell away in its entirety.   They were drowned in the absolute Unitude, and their intelligences were lost in its abyss " (p. [19]) ; and when they return to earthly illusions again from that world of reality they " confess with one voice that they had seen *nought existent* there save the One Real (Allāh) ".   *Existent* !   Do words mean what they say ?

No, not precisely ! with a Ghazzālī, and with Mohammedan mystics, clinging desperately to orthodoxy !   The matter, in fact, turns precisely on this word " existent ".   What *is* existence ?   What *is* non-existence ?   It was Ghazzālī's ontological philosophy that seems to have yielded him a fulcrum on which he could precariously balance the pantheistic and the deistic moments of his religious thought.

This philosophy is poetically stated in our treatise, but

---

[1] Which, it must be remembered, might not unfairly be translated " I am God " ; see footnote above.

in spite of the poetic, imaginative diction it can be recognized as identical with his usual doctrine.[1] It will be found on pp. [17–19, 21, 22]. We have there a picturesque representation of a doctrine well known to the schoolmen of Islām, that Not-Being is a sort of dark limbo in which the Contingent awaits the creative word *Kun* " Be ! "—compared in this " Light "-treatise to a ray of light from the One Self-existing Being. Neither the Greeks nor the schoolmen could ever quite get over the feeling that, in predicating anything of Not-being or a Nonentity, in using the word " is " in a sentence with Not-being or a Nonentity as its subject, you have in some way ascribed, not existence, but a sort of quasi-being, to that subject. Hegel's solution was so to evacuate the category of mere, bare " Being " of all content, and to demonstrate its consequent total impoverishment and inanity, that it could be seen to be the equivalent of Not-being. This was impossible for the schoolmen, above all for Oriental schoolmen, even of the most contradictory schools, who regarded the category of " pure " being (they would never have said " mere ") as the sublimest and most radiant of all the categories, and the very object of the whole quest of life. But the obverse of the Hegelian paradox may nevertheless be seen in their ascription to contingent not-yet-being a sort of quasi-existence. The effect of the creative word was simply to turn this potential into actual being. Thus the universe, always contingent, indeed, but formerly potential-contingent, *now* became actual-contingent.

All this is schematized in *al-Mishkāt*. The limbo becomes Darkness (p. 17) ; the potential-contingent, Dark Things [2] ;

---

[1] See, for example, *Munqidh* and the Lesser *Maqnūn* (if that is Ghazzālī's).

[2] It is just here that, as it seems to the writer, the Philosophers with their Aristotelian doctrine of the eternity of ὕλη—the formless substrate of things—might well have forced a place for *their* thought, in spite of the Ghazzālian wrath against them and it. For when the dark " self-aspect " of these contingencies of the Theologians is considered, prior to their " existence " (p. [59]), is there much to choose between the eternal potentiality asserted of them by Ghazzālī, and the eternity asserted for *hyle* by the Philosophers ? Ghazzālī himself quotes a saying of Mohammed

the divine creator, the Sun ; the creative act, a Ray from
His real being, whereby a dark Nonentity flashes into being
and becomes an Entity, but an Entity that depends
continuously on the permanent illumination of that ray,
for in the Mohammedan creational scheme, at any rate,
Creator is equally capable of being Annihilator.

At this point Ghazzālī's tortured thought is greatly helped
out by the ambiguous word *wajh*, which has two senses, or
rather three, Face, Side, Aspect (logical). This gave him
a formula : it was not the first time, nor the last, that the
ambiguity of the chief word in a theological formula has been
welcome to all concerned. He could take the Koran texts
" *the Wajh of everything faces (muwajjah) to Him and is turned
in His direction* ", and " *Whithersoever they turn themselves,
there is the Wajh of Allāh* " ; and the *ḥadīth qudsī*, " *Everything
is a perishing thing except His Wajh* " ; and could then play
on the word. In ancient and mediaeval times the merest
plays on words were not considered figures of speech but
profundities of thought. Quibbles masqueraded as dis-
coveries. And so this word (*a*) enabled Ghazzālī to keep his
hold on creationism on the one hand, for *these* were " things "
sure enough, all turned towards the central Sun and dependent
for their existence on its creative light ; and there was also
the sound logical position, that under this aspect (*wajh*) of
relatedness these things have actual being (p. [18]). So the
actuality of the universe is saved, and the abyss of pantheism
is avoided. *And* (*b*), on the other hand, he could say to the

(p. [13]), on to which these Philosophers would eagerly have seized as
proving their point : " Allah created the creation in darkness, then sent an
effusion of His light upon it." For a man who was using this divine light-
emanation to typify the act of creation, of calling out of not-being to being,
it was dangerous surely to give, apparently, so powerful an indication as
this of a previous *creation* in " darkness " (= not-being in Ghazzālī's chosen
symbology). It might very well have been claimed by the Philosophers
that this creation-in-darkness is precisely their formless, chaotic *hyle*,
eternal as darkness is eternal before the light shines. The Philosophers
did pretend to prove their thesis from the Koran ; see Averroes' *Manāhij*,
ed. Müller, p. 13 (= Cairo ed. *Falsaʿat Ibn Rushd*, p. 12), where the
following texts are cited in support, S. 11, 9 ; 14, 49 ; 41, 10.

pantheistic Ṣūfī (and to himself in that mood), that equally under this " aspect " of relatedness things, if and when considered *an sich*, had no existence, were not existent at all. The only Existent was the *Wajh Allāh* (p. [22]), that is, Allāh Himself, for, as he carefully informs us (p. [19]), Allāh cannot possibly be said to be " greater " (*akbar*) than His own *wajh* ; and must, therefore, be identical therewith.   And thus the out-and-out pantheist might well feel his case complete ; the last vestige of dualism disappears ; Allāh is All, and All is Allāh, *lā mawjūda ill-Allāh* (M., p. [18]) !   As Ghazzālī himself put it, Allāh is the Sun and besides the sun there is only the sun's light.   *Quid plura* ?

Nevertheless, it may be believed that Ghazzālī himself contrived to use this ontology so as to *keep*, not lose, his hold on the reality [1] and actuality of things, and that early training, central theological orthodoxy, and strong common-sense proved by its help too strong for the pull towards pantheism, with which his late Ṣūfism with its Neoplatonic atmosphere and sensational ecstasies undoubtedly did pull him—as Ṣūfism pulled every Mohammedan mystical devotee.   Is it not notable that even in the lyrical passages in this treatise, in which he describes (with a rather scared unction) the Mystics' intoxication and the verbal blasphemies which that state so happily permitted, and which were permitted to that state, Ghazzālī keeps his head, and preserves the same cautious balance as he does in the ontological sections (see pp. [19, 20]) ?   When these inebriates, he says, became sober again, " and they came under the sway of the intelligence . . . they knew that that had not been actual *Identity*, but only something resembling Identity " (not *homoousion* but *homoiousion* !).   If we correctly translate *ittiḥād* [2] thus, the remark is of crucial importance ; for the ultimate test of

---

[1] i.e. in the modern or western sense of the word, = " objectivity ".   To the mediaeval eastern thinker the Arabic word meant rather " ideality ".   It is a case of the difference between phenomenal and transcendental reality.

[2] Professor Macdonald prefers " identification ", to bring out the verbaspect of the *maṣdar* more clearly.

a complete Pantheism is whether things are *identical* with God, or only *united* with Him. All classes of mystics without exception assert at least the latter—it is the " Union " of the Christian, as of the Muslim, Catholic ; but only those who have actually surrendered their balance and toppled over into the pantheistic abyss assert the former. And Ghazzālī did not do so. He goes on to quote yet another " drunken " cry of a soul in Union, " I am He whom I love, and He whom I love is I," and shows how even here a distinction is preserved. And then that other, who likened the Union to a transparent Glass filled with red Wine—

> "The glass is thin, the wine is clear.
> The twain are alike, the matter is perplexed :
> For 'tis as though there were wine and no wine-glass there,
> Or as though there were wine-glass and nought of wine."

And thus comments : " Here there is a difference between saying ' The wine *is* the wine-glass ' and ' 'tis *as though it were* the wine-glass '." The former, he tells us, is *Identity* (*ittīḥād*), the latter *Unification* (*tawḥīd*), not in the commonalty's meaning of *tawḥīd*, he honestly says (p. [20]), for *them* this is one of " the mysteries which we are not at liberty to discuss "—but at the same time not inconsistent with that meaning. What he had in mind was, perhaps, something like this: " I reject the herd's interpretation of *tawḥīd*, the mere declaration-of-the-oneness of Allāh, as a bare truism, miserable in its inadequacy. I likewise reject the other extreme, the pantheist's interpretation of the word as an absolute denial of the actuality of things, or an assertion that things are Allāh. Against them both I assert that Allāh and the Universe constitute a UNITY, but one wherein the Universe is wholly relative to and dependent on Allāh, for existence or non-existence; preservation or annihilation. All existing things are and must be ' united ' to Allāh. But even this must not be declared openly, for, then, what about Iblis, Hell, and the Damned ? I must not seem to teach ' universalism ' any more than pantheism. *Allāhu a'lam* ! "

It therefore seems to the writer that Ghazzālī's position, which he tortured rather than explained when he tried to describe and illustrate it, really amounted to nothing more than the inevitable distinction between absolute and relative being ; between things when viewed relationally, in their relation to their Author, and things viewed apart from that relation. Neither Author nor Things were to be denied actuality, or reality, as we understand the latter term. As between Allāh and human intelligences he even goes great lengths (in this very treatise of all others) in asserting parallelism and comparability, similarity therefore [1] ; *but* between *Allāh* and all else ONE fundamental all-sufficient difference had to be asserted ; namely, ALLĀH is *self-subsistent, qayyūm* ; things are *not* so. This distinction was the minimum one ; yet also the maximum, for it preserved at once Creator and created, and gave actuality to each. There is, in truth, a good deal of wilful paradox in the *Mishkāt*, of Oriental hyperbole, of pious highfalutin,[2] *intended* perhaps to scare the " unco " orthodox of the day, to make their flesh creep a little for their health's sake, and to " wake them out of their dogmatic slumbers ". For it is in the *Mishkāt* that we find the following words, too, which seem plain and harmless enough : " Being is itself divided into that which has being-in-itself, and that which derives its being from not-itself. The being of this latter is borrowed, having no existence by itself. Nay, if it is regarded in and by itself it is pure not-being. *Whatever being it has* is due to its relation to not-itself, which is not real being at all . . ." In other words, it is by a purely arbitrary mental abstraction that we " regard derived being in and by itself ". The impossibility of really *effecting* this abstraction is precisely what preserves to derived

---

[1] And to assert similarity between two things is at once to have asserted *two*, and a distinction between them. See M., p. [7].

[2] Is not this true for *all* Ṣūfī writers ? Do we not take their language too seriously ? It parades as scientific ; it is really poetico-rhetorical.

being its measure of actuality—"whatever being it has　　" [1]
To *us* these last words are a clear concession of reality to
conditioned being.　It is true Ghazzālī denies reality to it
in the next sentence.　But this only shows that when an
Oriental talks of " Real " he means what we mean by " Un-
conditioned ", and that when he is thinking of " Conditioned or Relative " he says " Unreal ".　The matter has
become one of terms.

It is impossible to demand more than this from Ghazzālī
as philosopher-theologian.　He was, perhaps, not more
successful than other eastern theologians in finding a place
for the universe, philosophically, with or in Allāh.　But has
western philosophy been any more successful in finding a place
for Allāh, philosophically, with or in the universe ?

---

[1] Gh. has no more use for the Noumenon, for the *Ding an sich*, than had
the post-Kantians ; though for how different reasons !

TRANSLATION

[The references in square brackets are to the pages of the Cairo Arabic edition.]

THE NICHE FOR LIGHTS
(*Mishkāt al-Anwār*)

Praise to ALLĀH ! *who poureth forth light* ; *and giveth sight* ; *and, from His mysteries' height, removes the veils of night* !

And Prayer for MOHAMMED ! *of all lights the Light* ; *Sire of them that do the right* ; *Beloved of The Sovereign of Might* ; *Evangelist of the forgiven in His sight* ; *to Him devoted quite* ; *to sinner and to infidel the Arm that knows to fight and smite* !

You have asked me, dear brother—and may Allāh decree for you the quest of man's chiefest bliss, make you candidate for the Ascent to the highest height, anoint your vision with the light of Reality, and purge your inward parts from all that is not the Real !—you have asked me, I say, to communicate to you the mysteries of the Lights Divine, together with the allusions behind the literal meaning of certain texts in the Koran and certain sayings in the Traditions.

And principally this text [1] :—

" Allāh is the Light of the Heavens and of the Earth. The similitude of His Light is as it were a Niche wherein is a **Lamp** : *the Lamp within a Glass : the Glass as it were a pearly Star. From a Tree right blessed is it lit, an Olive-tree neither of the East nor of the West, the Oil whereof were well-nigh luminous though Fire touched it not : Light upon Light !*

" But as for the Infidels, their deeds are as it were massed Darkness upon some fathomless sea, the which is overwhelmed with billow topped by billow topped by cloud : Darkness on Darkness piled ! so that when a man putteth forth his hand he

---

[1] The Light-Verse in S. 24, 35. The Darkness-Verse, which almost immediately follows, and is mentioned in the exposition, has been added.

well-nigh can see it not. Yea, the man for whom Allāh doth not cause light, no light at all hath he."

What is the significance of His comparison of LIGHT with Niche, and Glass, and Lamp, and Oil, and Tree ?

And this Tradition :—

" Allāh hath Seventy Thousand Veils of Light and Darkness : were He to withdraw their curtain, then would the splendours of His Aspect [1] surely consume everyone who apprehended Him with his sight."

Such is your request. But in making it you have assayed to climb an arduous ascent, so high that the height thereof cannot be so much as gauged by mortal eyes [3]. You have knocked at a locked door which is only opened to those who know and *" are established in knowledge "*.[2] Moreover, not every mystery is to be revealed or divulged ; not every truth is to be laid bare or made plain, but—

"Noble hearts seal mysteries like the tomb."

Or, as one of those who Know has said—

"To divulge the secret of the Godhead is to deny God."

Or, as the prophet has said—

"There is a knowledge like the form of a hidden thing, known to none save those who know God."

If then these speak of that secret, only the Children of Ignorance will contradict them. And h   these Ignorants be, the Mysteries must from the gaze of sinners be kept inviolate.

But I believe that your heart has been opened by the Light and your consciousness purged of the darkness of Ignorance. I will, therefore, not be so niggardly as to deny you direction to these glorious truths in all their fineness and all their divineness ; for the wrong done in keeping Wisdom from her Children is not less than that of yielding her to those who are Strangers to her. As the poet hath it—

"He who bestoweth Knowledge on fools loseth it,
And he who keepeth the deserving from her doeth a wrong."

---

[1] Or Countenance ; see Introduction, p. 37.   [2] Cf. S. 3, 6.

You must, however, be content with a very summarized explanation of the subject; for the full demonstration of my theme would demand a treatment of both its principles and its parts for which my time is at present insufficient, and for which neither my mind nor my energies are free. The keys of all hearts are in the hands of Allāh: He opens them when He pleases, as He pleases, and with what He pleases. At this time, then, it shall suffice to open up to you three chapters or parts, whereof the first is as hereunder follows.

Part I.—LIGHT, AND LIGHTS: PRELIMINARY STUDIES

1. "Light" as Physical Light; as the Eye; as the Intelligence

The Real Light is Allāh; and the name " light " is otherwise only predicated metaphorically and conveys no real meaning.

To explain this theme: you must know that the word light is employed with a threefold signification: the first [4] by the Many, the second by the Few, the third by the Fewest of the Few. Then you must know the various grades of light that relate to the two latter classes, and the degrees of reality appertaining to these grades, in order that it may be disclosed to you, as these grades become clear, that ALLĀH is the highest and the ultimate Light: and further, as the reality appertaining to each grade is revealed, that Allāh *alone* is the Real, the True Light, and beside Him there is no light at all.

Take now the first signification. Here the word light indicates a *phenomenon*. Now a phenomenon, or appearance, is a relative term, for a thing necessarily appears to, or is concealed from, something other than itself; and thus its appearance and its non-appearance are both relative. Further, its appearance and its non-appearance are relative to *perceptive faculties*; and of these the most powerful and the most conspicuous, in the opinion of the Many, are the *senses,* one of which is the sense of *sight.* Further, things in relation to this sense of sight fall under three categories : (1) that which by itself is not visible, as dark bodies ; (2) that which is by itself visible, but cannot make visible anything else, such as luminaries like the stars, and fire before it blazes up ; (3) that which is by itself visible, and also makes visible, like the sun and the moon, and fire when it blazes up, and lamps. Now it is in regard to this third category that the name " light " is given : sometimes to that which is effused from these luminaries and falls on the exterior of opaque bodies, as when we say " The earth is lighted up ", or " The light of the sun falls on the earth ", or " The lamp-light falls on wall or on garment " ; and sometimes to the luminaries themselves, because they are self-luminous. In sum, then, light is an expression for that which *is by itself visible and* [5] *makes other things visible,* like the sun. This is the definition of, and the reality concerning light, according to its first signification.

We have seen that the very essence of light is appearance to a percipient ; and that perception depends on the existence of two things—light and a seeing eye. For, though light is that which appears and causes-to-appear, it neither appears nor causes-to-appear to the blind. Thus percipient spirit is as important as perceptible light *quâ* necessary element of perception : nay, 'tis the more important, in that it is the percipient spirit which apprehends, and through which apprehension takes place ; whereas light is not apprehensive, neither does apprehension take place through it, but merely when it is present. By the word light, in fact, is more properly understood that visualizing light which we call the eye. Thus men apply the word light to the light of the eye, and say of the weak-sighted that " *the light of his eye* is weak ", and of the blear-eyed that " *the light of his vision* is impaired ", and of the blind that " *his light* is quenched ". Similarly of the pupil of the eye it is said that it concentrates " the light " of vision, and strengthens it, the eye-lashes being given by the divine wisdom a black colour, and made to compass the eye every way round about, in order to concentrate its " light ". And of the white of the eye it is said that it disperses the " light of the eye " and weakens it, so that to look long at a bright white surface, or still more at the sun's light, dazzles " the light of the eye " and effaces it, just as the weak are effaced by the side of the strong. You understand, then, that percipient spirit is called light; and why it is so called ; and why it is more properly so called. And this is the second signification, that employed by the Few.

You must know, further, that the light of physical sight is [6] marked by several kinds of defects. It sees others but not itself. Again, it does not see what is very distant, nor what is very near, nor what is behind a veil. It sees the exterior of things only, not their interior ; the parts, not the whole ; things finite, not things infinite. It makes many mistakes in its seeing, for what is large appears to its vision small ; what is far, near ; what is at rest, at motion ; what is in motion, at rest. Here are seven defects inseparably attached to the physical eye. If, then, there be such an Eye as is free from all these physical defects, would not *it*, I ask, more properly be given the name of light ? Know, then, that there *is* in the mind of man an eye, characterized by just this perfection—that which is variously called Intelligence, Spirit, Human Soul. But we pass over these terms, for the multiplicity of the terms deludes the man of small intelligence into imagining a corresponding multiplicity of ideas. We mean simply that by which the rational man is distinguished from the infant in arms, from the brute beast, and from the lunatic. Let us call it *the Intelligence*, following the current terminology. So, then, the intelligence is more properly called Light than is the eye, just because in capacity it transcends these seven defects.

Take the first. The eye does not behold *itself*, but the intelligence does perceive itself as well as others ; and it perceives itself as endowed with knowledge, power, etc., and perceives its own knowledge and perceives its knowledge of its own knowledge, and its knowledge of its knowledge of its own knowledge, and so on *ad infinitum*. Now, this is a property which cannot conceivably be attributed to anything which perceives by means of a physical instrument like the eye. Behind this, however, [7] lies a mystery the unfolding of which would take long.

Take, now, the second defect : the eye does not see what is very near to it nor what is very far away from it ; but to the intelligence near and far are indifferent. In the twinkling of an eye it ascends to the highest heaven above, in another instant to the confines of earth beneath. Nay, when the facts are realized, intelligence is revealed as transcending the very idea of " far " and " near ", which occur between material bodies ; these compass not the precincts of its holiness, for it is a pattern or sample of the attributes of Allāh. Now the sample must be commensurate with the original, even though it does not rise to the degree of equality [1] with it. And this may move you to set your mind to work upon the true meaning of the tradition : " *Allāh created Adam after His own likeness.*" But I do not think fit at the present time to go more deeply into the same.

The third defect : the eye does not perceive what is behind the veil, but the intelligence moves freely about the Throne, the Sedile, and everything beyond the veil of the Heavens, and likewise about the Host Supernal, and the Realm Celestial, just as much as about its own world, and its propinquate, (that is its own) kingdom. The realities of things stand unveiled to the intelligence. Its only veil is one which it assumes of its own accord and for its own sake, which resembles the veil that the eye assumes of its own accord in the closing of its eyelids. But we shall explain this more fully in the third chapter of this work.

---

[1] Reading مساواة, which both sense and rhyme demand.

The fourth defect : the eye perceives only the exterior surfaces of things, but not their interior ; nay, the mere moulds and forms, not the realities ; while intelligence breaks through into the inwardness of things and into their secrets ; apprehends the reality of things and their essential spirit ; [8] elicits their causes and laws—from what they had origin, how they were created, of how many ideal forms they are composed, what rank of Being they occupy, what is their several relation to all other created things, and much else, the exposition of which would take very long ; wherein I think good to be brief.

The fifth : the eye sees only a fraction of what exists, for all concepts, and many percepts, are beyond its vision ; neither does it apprehend sounds, nor yet smells, nor tastes, nor sensations of hot and cold, nor the percipient faculties, by which I mean the faculties of hearing, of smelling, of tasting ; nay, all the inner psychical qualities are unseen to it, joy, pleasure, displeasure, grief, pain, delight, love, lust, power, will, knowledge, and innumerable other existences. Thus it is narrow in its scope, limited in its field of action, unable to pass the confines of the world of colour and form, which are the grossest of all entities ; for natural bodies are in themselves the grossest of the categories of being,.and colour and form are the grossest of their properties.   But the domain of intelligence is the entirety of existence, for it both apprehends the entities we have enumerated, and has free course among all others beside (and they are the major part), passing upon them judgments that are both certain and true.   To it, therefore, are the inward secrets of things manifest, and the hidden forms of things clear.   Then tell me by what right the physical eye is given equality with the intelligence in claiming the name of Light ?   No verily ! it is only relatively light ;   but in relation to the intelligence it is darkness. Sight is but one of the spies of Intelligence [9] who sets it to watch the grossest of his treasures, namely, the treasury of colours and forms ;   bids it carry reports about the same to its Lord, who then judges thereof in accordance with the dictates of his penetration and his judgment. Likewise are all the other faculties but Intelligence's spies—imagination, phantasy, thought, memory, recollection; and behind them are servitors and retainers, constrained to his service in this present world of his. These, I say, he constrains, and among these he moves at will, as freely as monarch constrains his vassals to his service, yea, and more freely still. But to expound this would take us long, and we have already treated of it in the book of my *Ihyā' al-'Ulūm*, entitled " The Marvels of the Mind ".

The sixth : the eye does not see what is infinite. What it sees is the attributes of known bodies, and these can only be conceived as finite. But the intelligence apprehends concepts, and concepts cannot be conceived as finite. True, in respect of the knowledge which has actually been attained, the content actually presented to the intelligence is no more than finite, but potentially it does apprehend that which is infinite. It would take too long to explain this fully, but if you desire an example, here is one from arithmetic. In this science the intelligence apprehends the series of integers, which series is infinite ; further, it apprehends the coefficients of two, three, and all the other integers, and to these also no limit can be conceived ; and it apprehends all the different relations between numbers, and to these also no limit can be conceived ; and finally it apprehends its own knowledge of a thing, and its knowledge of its knowledge of that thing, and its knowledge of its knowledge of its knowledge of that thing ; and so on, potentially, to infinity.

The seventh : the eye apprehends the large as small. It sees the sun the size of a bowl, and the stars like silver-pieces scattered upon a carpet of azure. But intelligence apprehends that the stars [10] and the sun are larger, times upon times, than the earth. To the eye the stars seem to be standing still, and the boy to be getting no taller. But the intelligence sees the boy moving constantly as he grows ;

the shadow lengthening constantly ; and the stars moving every instant, through distances of many miles. As the Prophet said to Gabriel, asking : " Has the sun moved ? " And Gabriel answered : " No—Yes." " How so ? " asked he ; and the other replied : " Between my saying No and Yes it has moved a distance equal to five hundred years." And so the mistakes of vision are manifold, but the intelligence transcends them all.

Perhaps you will say, we see those who are possessed of intelligence making mistakes nevertheless. I reply, their imaginative and phantastic faculties often pass judgments and form convictions which they think are the judgments of the intelligence. The error is therefore to be attributed to those lower faculties. See my account of all these faculties in my *Mī'ār al-'Ilm* and *Maḥakk al-Naẓar*. But when the intelligence is separated from the deceptions of the phantasy and the imagination, error on its part is inconceivable ; it sees things as they are. This separation is, however, difficult, and only attains perfection after death. Then is error unveiled, and then are mysteries brought to light, and each one meets the weal or the woe which he has already laid up for himself, and "*beholds a Book, which reckons each venial and each mortal sin, without omitting a single one* ".[1] In that hour it shall be said unto him : "*We have stripped from thee the Veil that covered thee and thy vision this day is iron.*"[2] Now that covering Veil is even that of the imagination and the phantasy ; and therefore the man who has been deluded by his own fancies, his false beliefs, and his vain imaginations, replies : "*Our Lord ! We have seen Thee and heard Thee !* [11] *O send us back and we will do good.*[3] *Verily now we have certain knowledge !* "

From all which you understand that *the eye* may more justly be called Light than the light (so called) which is apprehended by sense ; and further that *the intelligence* should more properly be called Light than the eye. It would be

---

[1] S. 50, 18.   [2] S. 22, 50.   [3] S. 12, 32.

even true to say that between these two there exists so great a difference in value, that we may, nay we must, consider only the INTELLIGENCE as deserving the name Light at all.

2. The Koran as the Sun of the Intelligence

Further you must notice here, that while the intelligence of men does truly see, the things it sees are not all upon the same plane. Its knowledge is in some cases, so to speak, *given*, that is, present in the intelligence, as in the case of axiomatic truths, e.g. that the same thing cannot be both with and without an origin ; or existent and non-existent ; or that the same proposition cannot be both true and false ; or that the judgment which is true of one thing is true of an identically similar thing ; or that, granted the existence of the particular, the existence of the universal must necessarily follow.

For example, granted the existence of black, the existence of " colour " follows ; and the same with " man " and " animal " ; but the converse does not present itself to the intelligence as necessarily true ; for " colour " does not involve " black ", nor does " animal " involve " man ". And there are many other true propositions, some necessary, some contingent, and some impossible. Other propositions, again, do not find the intelligence invariably with them, when they recur to it, but have to shake it up, arouse it, strike flint on steel, in order to elicit its spark. Instances of such propositions are the theorems of speculation, to apprehend which the intelligence has to be aroused by the dialectic (*kalām*) of the philosophers. Thus it is when the light of philosophy dawns that man sees actually, after having before seen potentially. Now the greatest [12] of philosophies is the word (*kalām*) of Allāh in general, and the Koran in particular.

Therefore the verses of the Koran, in relation to intelligence, have the value of sunlight in relation to the eyesight, to wit, it is by this sunlight that the act of seeing is accomplished.

And therefore the Koran is most properly of all called Light, just as the light of the sun is called light. The Koran, then, is represented to us by the Sun, and the intelligence by the Light of the Eye, and hereby we understand the meaning of the verse, which saith : " *Believe then on Allāh and His Prophet, and the Light which we caused to descend* " [1] ; and again : " *There hath come a sure proof from your Lord, and we have caused a clear Light to descend.*" [2]

3. The Worlds Visible and Invisible : with their Lights

You have now realized that there are two kinds of eye, an external and an internal ; that the former belongs to one world, the World of Sense, and that internal vision belongs to another world altogether, the World of the Realm Celestial ; and that each of these two eyes has a sun and a light whereby its seeing is perfected ; and that one of these suns is external, the other internal, the former belonging to the seen world, viz. the sun, which is an object of sense-perception, and the other internal, belonging to the world of the Realm Celestial, viz. the Koran, and other inspired books of Allāh. If, then, this has been disclosed to you thoroughly and entirely, then one of the doors of this Realm Celestial has been opened unto you. In that world there are marvels, in comparison with which this world of sight is utterly contemned. He who never fares to that world, but allows the limitations of life in this lower world of sense to settle upon him, is still a brute-beast, an excommunicate from that which constitutes us men ; gone astray is he more than any brute beast, for to the brute are not vouched the wings of flight, on which to fly away unto that invisible world. " *Such men,*" the Koran says, " *are cattle, nay, are yet further astray !* " [3] [13] As the rind is to the fruit ; as the mould or the form in relation to the spirit ; as darkness in relation to light ; as infernal to supernal ; so is this World of Sense in relation to the world

---

[1] S. 64, 8.   [2] S. 4, 173.   [3] S. 7, 178.

of the Realm Celestial. For this reason the latter is called the World Supernal or the World of Spirit, or the World of Light, in contrast with the World Beneath, the World of Matter and of Darkness. But do not imagine that I mean by the World Supernal the World of the [Seven] Heavens, though they are " above " in respect of part of our world of sense-perception. *These* heavens are equally present to our apprehension, and that of the lower animals. But a man finds the doors of the Realm Celestial closed to him, neither does he become of or belonging to that Realm unless " *this earth to him be changed into that which is not earth, and likewise the heavens* "[1] ; unless, in short, all that comes within the ken of his sense and his imagination, including the visible heavens, cease to be his earth, and his heaven come to be all that transcends his sense. This is the first Ascension for every Pilgrim, who has set out on his Progress to approach the Presence Dominical. Thus mankind was consigned back to the lowest of the low, and must thence rise to the world of highest height. Not so is it with the Angels ; for they are part of the World of the Realm Celestial, floating ever in the Presence of the Transcendence, whence they gaze down upon our World Inferior. Thereof spoke the Prophet in the Tradition: " *Allāh created the creation in darkness, then sent an effusion of His light upon it,*" and " *Allāh hath Angels, beings who know the works of men better than they know them themselves* ". Now the Prophets, when their ascents reached unto the World of the Realm Celestial, attained the uttermost goal, and from thence looked down upon a totality of the World Invisible ; for he who is in the World of the Realm Celestial is with Allāh, and hath the keys [14] of the Unseen. I mean that from where he is the causes of existing things descend into the World of Sense; for the world of sense is one of the effects of yonder world of cause, resulting from it just as the shadow results from a body, or as fruit from that which fructuates, or as the effect from a cause. Now the

[1] S. 14, 48.

key to this knowledge of the effect is sought and found in the cause. And for this reason the World of Sense is a type of the World of the Realm Celestial, as will appear when we explain the NICHE, the LAMP, and the TREE. For the thing compared is in some sort parallel, and bears resemblance, to the thing compared therewith, whether that resemblance be remote or near : a matter, again, which is unfathomably deep, so that whoever has scanned its inner meaning has had revealed to him the verities of the types in the Koran by an easy way.

I said that everything that sees self and not-self deserves more properly the name of Light, while that which adds to these two functions the function of making the not-self visible, still more properly deserves the name of Light than that which has no effect whatever beyond itself. *This* is the light which merits the name of " *Lamp Illuminant* ",[1] because its light is effused upon the not-self. Now this is the property of the transcendental prophetic spirit, for through its means are effused the illuminations of the sciences upon the created world. Thus is explained the name given by Allāh to Mohammed, " *Illuminant.*" [2] Now all the Prophets are Lamps, and so are the Learned—but the difference between them is incalculable.

4. These Lights as Lamps Terrestrial and Celestial : with their Order and Grades

If it is proper to call that from which the light of vision emanates a " Lamp Illuminant ", then that from which the Lamp is itself lit may [15] meetly be symbolized by *Fire*. Now all these Lamps Terrestrial were originally lit from the Light Supernal alone ; and of the transcendental Spirit of prophecy it is written that " *Its oil were well-nigh luminous though fire touched it not* "; but becomes " *very light upon light* " when touched by that Fire.[3] Assuredly, then, the kindling

---

[1] S. 33, 46.   [2] S. 46, 33.
[3] S. 24, 35; see p. [45] of translation.

source of those Spirits Terrestrial is the divine Spirits Supernal, described by Ali and Ibn Abbas, when they said that " Allāh hath an Angel with countenances seventy thousand, to each countenance seventy thousand mouths, in each mouth seventy thousand tongues wherewith he laudeth God most High ". This is he who is contrasted with all the angelic host, in the words : " *On the day whereon* THE SPIRIT *ariseth, and the Angels, rank on rank.*" [1] These Spirits Celestial, then, if they be considered as the kindling-source of the Lamps Terrestrial, can be compared alone with "*Fire*".[2] And that kindling is not perceived save " *on the Mountain's side* ".[3]

Let us now take these Lights Celestial from which are lit the Lamps Terrestrial, and let us rank them in the order in which they themselves are kindled, the one from the other. Then the nearest to the fountain-head will be of all others the worthiest of the name of Light, for he is the highest in order and rank.   Now the analogy for this graded order in the world of sense can only be seized by one who sees the light of the moon coming through the window of a house, falling on a mirror fixed upon a wall, which reflects that light on to another wall, whence it in turn is reflected on to the floor, so that the floor becomes illuminated therefrom. The light upon the floor is owed to that upon the wall, and the light on the wall to that in the mirror, and the light in the mirror to that from the moon, and the light in the moon to that from the sun, [16] for it is the sun that radiates its light upon the moon. Thus these four lights are ranged one above the other, each one more perfect than the other ; and each one has a certain rank and a proper degree which it never passes beyond. I would have you know, then, that it has been revealed to the men of Insight that even so are the Lights of the Realm Celestial ranged in an order ; and that the highest is the one who is nearest to the Ultimate Light. It may well be, then, that the rank of Seraphiel is above the rank of Gabriel ; and that among them is that Nighest to Allāh, he whose rank

[1] S. 28, 78.   [2] S. 28, 29.   [3] S. 28, 29 ; also 19, 53.

comes nighest to the Presence Dominical which is the Fountain-head of all these lights ; and that among these is a Nighest to Man, and that between these two are grades innumerable, whereof all that is known is that they are many, and that they are ordered in rank and grade, and that as they have described themselves, so they are indeed—" *Not one of us but has his determined place and standing,*" [1] and " *We are verily the ranked ones ; we are they in whose mouth is Praise* ".[1]

5. The Source of all these Grades of Light : ALLAH

The next thing I would have you know is that these degrees of light do not ascend in an infinite series, but rise to a final Fountain-head who is Light in and by Himself, upon Whom comes no light from any external source, and from Whom every light is effused according to its order and grade. Ask yourself, now, whether the name Light is more due to that which is illumined and borrows its light from an external source ; or to that which in itself is luminous, illuminating all else beside ? I do not believe that you can fail to see the true answer, and thus conclude that the name light is most of all due to this LIGHT SUPERNAL, above Whom there is no light at all!, and from Whom light descends upon all other things.

Nay, I do not hesitate to say boldly that the term " light " as applied to aught else than this primary light is purely metaphorical ; for all [17] others, if considered in themselves, have, in themselves and by themselves, no light at all. Their light is borrowed from a foreign source , which borrowed illumination has not any support in itself, only in something not-itself. But to call the borrower by the same name as the lender is mere metaphor. Think you that the man who borrows riding-habit, saddle, horse, or other riding beast, and mounts the same when and as the lender appoints, is actually, or only metaphorically, rich ? Or is it the lender

---

[1] S. 37, 164–6.

who alone is rich ? The latter, assuredly ! The borrower remains in himself as poor as ever, and only of him who made the loan and exacts its return can richness be predicated—him who gave and can take away. Therefore, the Real Light is He in Whose hand lies creation and its destinies ; He who first gives the light and afterwards sustains it. He shares with no other the reality of this name, nor the full title to the same : save in so far as He calls some other by that name, deigns to call him by it in the same way as a Liege-Lord deigns to give his vassal a fief, and therewith bestows on him the title of lord. Now when that vassal realizes the truth, he understands that both he and his are the property of his Liege, and of Him alone, a property shared by Him with no partner in the world.

You now know that Light is summed up in *appearing* and *manifesting*, and you have ascertained the various gradations of the same. You must further know that there is no darkness so intense as the darkness of Not-being. For [1] a dark thing is called " dark " simply because it cannot appear to anyone's vision : it never comes to exist for sight, though it does exist in itself. But that which has no existence for others *nor* for itself is assuredly the very extreme of darkness. In contrast with it is Being, which is, therefore, Light ; for unless a thing is manifest in itself, [18] it is not manifest to others. Moreover, Being is itself divided into that which has being in itself, and that which derives its being from not-itself. The being of this latter is borrowed, having no existence by itself. Nay, if it is regarded in and by itself, it is pure not-being. Whatever being it has is due to its relation to a not-itself : and this is not real being at all, as you learned from my parable of the Rich and the Borrowed Garment. Therefore, Real Being is Allāh most High, even as Real Light is likewise Allāh.

<hr>

¹ Reading لَوْ for لَهُ.

6. The Mystic Verity of Verities

It is from this starting-point that Allāh's gnostics rise from metaphors to realities, as one climbs from the lowlands to the mountains ; and at the end of their Ascent see, as with the direct sight of eye-witnesses, that there is nothing in existence save Allāh alone, and that "*everything perisheth except His Countenance, His Aspect*" [1] (*wajh*) ; not that [2] it perisheth at some particular moment, but rather it is sempiternally a perishing thing, since it cannot be conceived except as perishing. For each several thing other than Allāh is, when considered in and by itself, pure not-being ; and if considered from the " aspect " (*wajh*) to which existence flows from the Prime Reality, it is viewed as existing, but not in itself, solely from the " aspect " which accompanies Him Who gives it existence. Therefore, the God-aspect is the sole thing in existence. For everything has two aspects, an aspect to itself and an aspect to its Lord : in respect of the first, it is Not-being ; but in respect of the God-aspect, it is Being. *Therefore* there is no Existent except God and the God-aspect, and therefore all things are perishing except the God-aspect from and to all eternity. These gnostics, therefore, have no need to await the arising of the Last Uprising in order to hear the Creator proclaim, " *To whom is the power this day ? To* ALLĀH ! *the One, the Not-to-be-withstood* " [3] ; [19] for that summons is pealing in their ears always and for ever. Neither do they understand by the cry " Allāh is most great " (*Allāhu akbar*) that He is only " greater " than others. God forbid ! For in all existence there is beside Him none for Him to exceed in greatness. No other attains so much as to the degree of co-existence, or of sequent existence, nay of existence at all, except from the Aspect that accompanies Him. All existence is, exclusively, His Aspect. Now it is impossible that He should be " greater " than His own

---

[1] S. 88, 28.   [2] Reading اِلَّا.   [3] S. 16. 40.

Aspect.   The meaning is rather that he is too absolutely Great to be called Greater, or Most Great, by way of relation or comparison—too Great for anyone, whether Prophet or Angel, to grasp the real nature of His Greatness.   For none knows Allāh with a real knowledge but He Himself ; for every known falls necessarily under the sway and within the province of the Knower ; a state which is the very negation of all Majesty, all "Greatness ".   The full proof whereof I have given in my *al-Maqṣad al-Asnā fī maʿānī asmā'i-llāhi-l Ḥusnā*.

These gnostics, on their return from their Ascent into the heaven of Reality, confess with one voice that they saw nought existent there save the One Real.   Some of them, however, arrived at this scientifically, and others experimentally and subjectively.   From these last the plurality of things fell away in its entirety.   They were drowned in the absolute Unitude, and their intelligences were lost in Its abyss.   Therein became they as dumbfoundered things.   No capacity remained within them sav to recall ALLĀH ; yea, not so much as the capacity to recall their own selves.   So there remained nothing with them save ALLĀH.   They became drunken with a drunkenness wherein the sway of their own intelligence disappeared; so that one[1] exclaimed, " I am The ONE REAL ! " and another, " Glory be to ME !   How great is My glory ! "[2] and another, " Within this robe is nought but Allāh ! "[2] . . . .   But the words of Lovers Passionate in their intoxication and ecstacy [20] mu t be hidden away and not spoken of. . . .   Then when that drunkenness abated and they came again under the sway of the intelligence, which is Allāh's balance-scale upon earth, they knew that that had not been actual Identity, but only something resembling Identity :   as in those words of the Lover at the height of his passion :—

---

[1] Al-Ḥallāj.

[2] Abū Yazīd al-Bisṭāmī.   See Massignon's *Ḥallāj*, p. 513.

"I am He whom I love and He whom I love is I;
  We are two spirits immanent in one body."[1]

For it is possible for a man who has never seen a mirror in his life, to be confronted suddenly by a mirror, to look into it, and to think that the form which he sees in the mirror *is* the form of the mirror itself, " identical " with it. Another might see wine in a glass, and think that the wine is just the stain of the glass. And if that thought becomes with him use and wont, like a fixed idea with him, it absorbs him wholly, so that he sings :—

" The glass is thin, the wine is clear!
  The twain are alike, the matter is perplexed;
  For 'tis as though there were wine and no wine-glass there,
  Or as though there were wine-glass and nought of wine ! "

Here there is a difference between saying, " The wine *is* the wine-glass," and saying, " 'tis *as though it were* the wine-glass." Now, when this state prevails, it is called in relation to him who experiences it, Extinction, nay, Extinction of Extinction, for the soul has become extinct to itself, extinct to its own extinction ; for it becomes unconscious of itself and unconscious of its own unconsciousness, since, were it conscious of its own unconsciousness, it would be conscious of itself. In relation to the man immersed in this state, the state is called, in the language of metaphor, " Identity " ; in the language of reality, " Unification." And beneath these verities also lie mysteries which we are not at liberty to discuss.

7. The "God-Aspect": an "advanced" explanation of the relation of these Lights to ALLAH

It may be that you desire greatly to know the aspect (*wajh*) [21] whereby Allāh's light is related to the heavens and the earth, or rather the aspect whereby He is in Himself the Light of heavens and earth. And this shall assuredly not be denied you, now that you know that Allāh is Light, and that beside Him there is no light, and that He is every light, and

---

[1] By al-Hallāj.

that He is the universal light : since light is an expression
for that by which things are revealed ; or, higher still, that
by and for which they are revealed ; yea, and higher still,
that by, for, and from which they are revealed : and now that
you know, too that, of everything called light, only that by,
for, and from which things are revealed is *real*—that Light
beyond which there is no light to kindle and feed its flame,
for It is kindled and fed in Itself, from Itself, and for Itself,
and from no other source at all. Such a conception, such a
description, you are now assured, can be applied to the Great
Primary alone. You are also assured that the heavens and
the earth are filled with light appertaining to those two
fundamental light-planes, our *Sight* and our *Insight* ; by
which I mean our *senses* and our *intelligence*. The first kind
of light is what we see in the heavens--sun and moon and
stars ; and what we see in earth—that is, the rays which are
poured over the whole face of the earth, making visible all the
different colours and hues, especially in the season of spring ;
and over all animals and plants and things, in all their states :
for without these rays no colour would appear or even exist.
Moreover, every shape and size which is visible to perception
is apprehended in consequence of colour, and it is impossible
to conceive of apprehending them without colour. As for
the other ideal, intelligential Lights, the World Supernal is
filled with them—to wit, the angelic substances ; and the
World Inferior is also full of them—[22] to wit, animal life
and human life successively. The order of the World Inferior
is manifested by means of this inferior human light ; while the
order of the World Supernal is manifested by means of that
angelical light. This is the order alluded to in the passage
in the Koran, "*He it is Who has formed you from the earth,
and hath peopled it with you, that He might call you Successors
upon the earth*" . . . and "*Maketh you Successors on the
earth*", and "*Verily I have set in the earth a Successor*"
(*Khalīfa*).[1]

[1] S. 61, 11 ; 55, 24 ; 62, 27 ; 30, 2. Cf. *Mishkāt*, p. [34].

Thus you see that the whole world is all filled with the external lights of perception, and the internal lights of intelligence ; also that the lower lights are effused or emanate the one from the other, as light emanates or is effused from a lamp ; while the Lamp itself is the transcendental Light of Prophecy ; and that the transcendental Spirits of Prophecy are lit from the Spirit Supernal, as the lamp is lit from fire ; and that the Supernals are lit the one from the other ; and that their order is one of ascending grades : further, that these all rise to the Light of Lights, the Origin and Fountain-head of lights, and that is ALLĀH, only and alone ; and that all other lights are borrowed from Him, and that His alone is real light ; and that everything is from His light, nay, He is everything, nay, HE IS THAT HE IS, none but He has ipseity or heity at all, save by metaphor.   Therefore there is no light but He, while all other lights are only lights from the Aspect which accompanies Him, not from themselves.   Thus the aspect and face of everything faces to Him and turns in His direction ; and *"whithersoever they turn themselves there is the Face of Allāh"*.[1]   So, then, there is no divinity but HE ; for "*d*ivinity" is an expression by which is connoted that towards which all faces are "*d*irected"[2] in worship and in confession that He is Deity ; by which I mean the faces of the *hearts* of men, for they verily are lights and spirits.   Nay, more, just as " there is no *deity* but He ", so there is no *heity* but He, [23] for " he " is an expression for something which one can indicate ; but in every and any case we can but indicate HIM.   Every time you indicate anything, your indication is, in reality, to Him, even though through your ignorance of the truth of truths which we have mentioned you know it not.   Just as one cannot point to, indicate, *sunlight* but only the *sun*, so the relation of the sum of things to

---

[1] S. 2, 115, see 144, 149, 150.

[2] Gh.'s piece of amateur etymology here, by which he appears to derive the root *'lh* ("god") from the root *wly* ("turn"), is about as absurd as my attempt to suggest it in the English.

Allāh is, in the visible analogue, as the relation of light to the sun. Therefore " *There is no deity but* ALLĀH " is the Many's declaration of Unity : that of the Few is " *There is no he but* HE " ; the former is more general, but the latter is more particular, more comprehensive, more exact, and more apt to give him who declares it entrance into the pure and absolute Oneness and Onliness. This kingdom of the One-and-Onliness is the ultimate point of mortals' Ascent : there is no ascending stage beyond it ; for " ascending " involves plurality, being a sort of relativity involving two stages, an ascent *from* and an ascent *to*. But when Plurality has been eliminated, Unity is established, relation is effaced, all indication from " here " to " there " falls away, and there remains neither height nor depth, nor anyone to fare up or down. The upward Progress, the Ascent of the soul, then becomes impossible, for there is no height beyond the Highest, no plurality alongside of the One, and, now that plurality has terminated, no Ascent for the soul. If there be, indeed, any change, it is by way of the " Descent into the Lowest Heaven ", the radiation from above downwards ; for the Highest, though It may have no higher, has a lower. This is the goal of goals, the last object of spiritual search, known of him who knows it, denied by him who is ignorant of it. It belongs to that knowledge which is according to the form of the hidden thing, and which no one knoweth save the Learned [1] in Allāh. If, therefore, they utter it, it is only denied by the Ignorant of Him.

There is no improbability in the explanation given by these Learned to this " Descent into the Lowest Heaven ", [24] namely, that it is the descent of *an Angel* ; though one of those Gnostics [2] has, indeed, fancied a less probable explanation. He, immersed as he was in the divine One-and-Onliness, said that *Allāh* has " a descent into the lowest heaven ", and that this descent is *His* descent, in order to use physical senses, and to set in motion bodily limbs ; and that *He* is the

---

[1] Cf. S. 3, 7.   [2] Al-Ḥallāj.

one indicated in the Tradition in which the Prophet says, " *I have become His hearing whereby He heareth, His vision whereby He seeth, His tongue wherewith He speaketh.*" [1] Now if the Prophet was Allāh's hearing and vision and tongue, then *Allāh* and He alone is the Hearer, the Seer, the Speaker ; and *He* is the one indicated in His own word to Moses, " *I was sick, and thou visitedst ME not.*" [2] According to this, the bodily movements of this Confessor of the divine Unity are from the lowest heaven ; his sensations from a heaven next above ; and his intelligence from the heaven next above that. From that heaven of the intelligence he fares upward to the limit of the Ascension of created things, the kingdom of the One-and-Onliness, a sevenfold way ; thereafter " *settleth he himself on the throne*" of the divine Unity, and therefrom " *taketh command* " [3] throughout his storied heavens. Well might one, in looking upon such an one, apply to him the saying, " *Allāh created Adam after the image of the Merciful One* " ; until, after contemplating that word more deeply, he becomes aware that it has an interpretation like those other words, " I am the ONE REAL," " Glory be to ME ! " [4] or those sayings of the Prophet, that Allāh said, " *I was sick and thou visitedst ME not,*" and " *I am His hearing, and His vision, and His tongue* ". But I see fit now to draw rein in this exposition, for I think that you cannot bear more of this sort than the amount which I have now communicated.

8. The Relation of these Lights to ALLAH : Simpler Illustrations and Explanations

It may well be that you will not rise to the height of these words, for all your pains ; it may be that for all your pains you will come short of it after all. Here, then, is something that lies nearer your understanding, and nearer your weakness.

---

[1] A saying reported by Ibn Adham, d. 170.

[2] See St. Matt. xxv.

[3] Ar. *al amr.* See on p. [55], Introduction, pp. 18-22. Or, " controlleth things." And see S. 32, 5.

[4] M., p. [19].

The meaning of the doctrine that Allāh is [25] the Light of Heavens and Earth may be understood in relation to phenomenal, visible light. When you see hues of spring—the tender green, for example—in the full light of day, you entertain no doubt but that you are looking on colours, and very likely you suppose that you are looking on nothing else alongside of them. As though you should say, " I see nothing alongside of the green." Many have, in fact, obstinately maintained this. . They have asserted that light is a meaningless term, and that there *is* nothing but colour with the colours. Thus they denied the existence of the light, although it was the most manifest of all things—how should it not be so, considering that through it alone all things become manifest ?, for it is the thing that is itself visible and makes visible, as we said before. But, when the sun sank, and heaven's lamp disappeared from sight, and night's shadow fell, then apprehended these men the existence of an essential difference between inherent shadow and inherent light ; and they confessed that light is a form that lies behind all colour, and is apprehended with colour, insomuch that, so to speak, through its intense union with the colours it is not apprehended, and through its intense obviousness it is invisible. And it may be that this very intensity is the direct cause of its invisibility, for things that go beyond one extreme pass over to the extreme opposite.

If this is clear to you, you must further know that those endowed with this Insight never saw a single object without seeing Allāh along with it. It may be that one of them went further than this and said, " I have never seen a single object, but I first saw Allāh " ; for some of them only see objects through and in Allāh, while others first see objects and then see Allāh in and through those objects. It is to the first class that the Koran alludes to in the words, " *Doth it not suffice that thy Lord seeth all ?* " [1] and to the second in the words, " *We shall shew them our signs in all the world and in themselves.* " [1] For the first class [26] have the direct intuition

<hr>

[1] S. 41, 53.

of Allāh, and the second infer Him from His works.
The former is the rank of the Saint-Friends of God, the latter
of the Learned " *who are stablished in knowledge* ".[1] After
these two grades there remains nothing except that of the
careless, on whose faces is the veil.

Thus you see that just as everything is manifest to man's
Sight by means of light, so everything is manifest to man's
Insight by means of Allāh ; for He is *with* everything every
moment and by Him does everything appear. But here the
analogy ceases, and we have a radical difference ; namely,
that phenomenal light can be conceived of as disappearing
with the sinking of the sun, and as assuming a veil in order
that shadow may appear : while the divine light, which is the
condition of all appearance, cannot be conceived as disappearing. That sun can never set ! It abides for ever with
all things. Thus the method of difference (as a method for
the demonstration of the Existence of God from His works)
is not at our disposal. Were the disappearance of Allāh
conceivable, heaven and earth would fall to ruin, and thence,
through difference, would be apprehended an effect which
would simultaneously compel the recognition of the Cause
whereby all things appeared. But, as it is, all Nature remains
the same and invariable to our sight because of the unity of its
Creator, for " *all things are singing His praise* "[2] (not some
things) at *all* times (not sometimes) ; and thus the method
of difference is eliminated, and the way to the knowledge of
God is obscured. For the most manifest way to the knowledge
of things is by their contraries : the thing that possesses no
contrary and no opposite, its features being always exactly
alike when you are looking at it, will very likely elude your
notice altogether. In this case its obscureness results from
its very obviousness, and its elusiveness from the very radiance
of its brightness. Then glory to Him who hides Himself
from His own creation by His utter manifestness, and is

<hr>

[1] S. 3, 6.   [2] See S. 17, 44.

veiled from their gaze through the very effulgence of His own light !

But it may be that not even this teaching is intelligible to some limited intelligences, [27] who from our statement (that " Allāh is *with* everything ", as the light is with everything) will understand that He is in every *place*. Too high and holy is He to be related to place ! So far from starting this vain imagining, we assert to you that He is prior to everything, and above everything, and that He makes everything manifest. Now manifester is inseparable from manifested, subjectively, in the cognition of the thinker ; and this is what we mean by saying that Allāh accompanies or is " with " everything. You know, further, that manifester is prior to, and above, manifested, though He be " with " it ; but he is " with " it from one aspect, and " above " it from another. You are not to suppose, therefore, that there is here any contradiction. Or, consider, how in the world of sense, which is the highest to which your knowledge can rise, the motion of your hand goes " with " the motion of its shadow, and yet is prior to it as well. And whoever has not wit enough to see this, ought to abandon these researches altogether ; for

> " To every science its own people ;
>> And each man finds easy that for which he has been
>> created apt."

Part II.—THE SCIENCE OF SYMBOLISM
Prolegomena to the Explanation of the Symbolism of the ⁻Iche, the Lamp, the Glass, the Tree, the Oil, and the Fire

The exposition of this symbolism involves, first of all, two cardinal considerations, which afford limitless scope for investigation, but to which I shall merely allude very briefly here.

First, the science and method of symbolism ; the way in

which the spirit of the ideal form [1] is captured by the mould
of the symbol; the mutual relationship of the two; the inner
nature of this correspondence between the world of Sense
(which supplies the clay of the moulds, the material of the
symbolism) and the world of the Realm Supernal from which
the Ideas descend.[2]

Second, the gradations of the several spirits of our mortal
clay, and the degree [28] of light possessed by each. For
we treat of this latter symbolism in order to explain the former.

I. The Outward and the Inward in Symbolism : Type and Antitype

The world is Two Worlds, spiritual and material, or, if
you will, a World Sensual and a World Intelligential; or
again, if you will, a World Supernal and a World Inferior.
All these expressions are near each other, and the difference
between them is merely one of view-point. If you regard the
two worlds in themselves, you use the first expression ; if
in respect of the organ which apprehends them, the second ;
if in respect of their mutual relationship, the third.   You may,
perhaps, also term them the World of Dominance and Sense-
perception, and, the World of the Unseen and the Realm
Supernal. It were no marvel if the student of the realities
underlying the terminology were puzzled by the multiplicity
of these terms, and imagined a corresponding multiplicity of
ideas.   But he to whom the realities beneath the terms are
disclosed makes the ideas primary and the terms secondary :
while inferior minds take the opposite course. To them the
term is the source from which the reality proceeds.   We have
an allusion to these two types of mind in the Koran, " *Whether
is the more rightly guided, he who walks with his face bent down,
or he who walks in a straight Way, erect ?* " [3]

---

[1] Or Idea = ἰδέα, in practically the Platonic sense.

[2] (By Ghazzālī.)   In this Light-Verse, in Ibn Mas‘ūd's reading, the words
" in the heart of the believer " follow the words " of His light ".   And
Ubayy b. Ka‘b's, instead of " the similitude of His light ", has " the
similitude of the light of the heart of him who believes is like ", etc.

[3] S. 67, 22.

1. The Two Worlds : their types and antitypes

Such is the idea of the Two Worlds.   And the next thing for you to know is, that the supernal world of " the Realm " is a world invisible, for it is invisible to the majority of men ; and the world of our senses is the world of perception, because it is perceived of all.   This World Sensual is the point from which we ascend to [29] the world Intelligential ; and, but for this connexion between the two, and their reciprocal relationship, the Way upward to the higher sphere would be barred.   And were this upward way impossible, then would the Progress to the Presence Dominical and the near approach to Allāh be impossible too.   For no man shall approach near unto Allāh, unless his foot stand at the very centre of the Fold of the Divine Holiness.   Now by this World of the " Divine *Holiness* " we mean the world that *transcends* the apprehension of the senses and the imagination.   And it is in respect of the law of that world—the law that the soul which is a stranger to it neither goeth out therefrom, nor enteret therein—that we call it the Fold of the Divine Holiness and Transcendence.   And the human spirit. which is the channel of the manifestations of this Transcendence, may be perhaps called " *the Holy Valley* ".[1]

Again, this Fold comprises lesser folds, some of which penetrate more deeply than others into the ideas of the Divine Holiness.   But the term Fold embraces all the gradations of the lesser ones ; for you must not suppose that these terms are enigmas, unintelligible to men of Insight. But I cannot pursue the subject further, for I see that my preoccupation with citing and explaining all this terminology is turning me from my theme.   It is for you to apply yourself now to the study of the terms.

To return to the subject we were discussing : the visible world is, as we said, the point of departure up to the world of the Realm Supernal : and the " Pilgrim's Progress of the Straight Way "[2] is an expression for that upward course, which may

____
[1] S. 20, 12.   [2] See S. 1, 4.

also be expressed by " The Faith ", " the Mansions of Right
Guidance ".   Were there no relation between the two worlds,
no inter-connexion at all, then all upward progress would be
inconceivable from one to the other.   Therefore, the divine
mercy gave to the World Visible a correspondence with the
World of the Realm Supernal, and for this reason there is not
a single thing in this world of sense that it not a symbol of
something in yonder one.   It may well hap that some one
thing in this world may symbolize several things in the World
of the Realm Supernal, and equally well that some one thing
in the latter may have several symbols [30] in the World
Visible.   We call a thing typical or symbolic when it resembles
and corresponds to its antitype under some aspect.

A complete enumeration of these symbols would involve our
exhausting the whole of the existing things in both of the Two
Worlds !   Such a task our mortal powers can never fulfil ;
our human faculties have not sufficed to comprehend it in the
past ; and with our little lives we cannot expound it fully in
the present.   The utmost I can do is to explain to you a single
example.   The greater may then be inferred from the less ;
for the door of research into the mysteries of this knowledge
will then lie open to you.

2. An Example of Symbolism, from the Story
of Abraham in the Koran

Listen now.   If the World of the Realm Supernal contains
Light-substances, high and lofty, called " Angels ", from which
substances the various lights are effused upon the various
mortal spirits, and by reason of which these angels are called
" lords ", then is Allāh " Lord of lords ", and these lords will
have differing grades of luminousness.   The symbols, then,
of these in the visible world will be, pre-eminently, the Sun,
the Moon, and the Stars.   And the Pilgrim of the Way rises
first of all to a degree corresponding to that of a *star*.   The
effulgence of that star's light appears to him.   It is disclosed
to him that the entire world beneath adores its influence and

the effulgence of its light. And so, because of the very beauty and superbness of the thing. he is made aware of something which cries aloud saying, " *This is my Lord!* " [1] He passes on ; and as he becomes conscious of the light-degree next above it, namely, that symbolized by *the moon*, lo ! in the aerial canopy he beholds that star set, to wit, in comparison with its superior ; and he saith, " *Nought that setteth do I adore!* " And so he rises till he arrives at last at the degree symbolized by *the sun*. This, again, he sees is greater and higher than the former, but nevertheless admits of comparison therewith, in virtue of a relationship between the two. [31] But to bear relationship to what is imperfect carries with it imperfection—the " setting " of our allegory. And by reason thereof he saith : " *I have turned my face unto That Who made the heavens and the earth ! I am a true believer, and not of those who associate other gods with Allāh !* " Now what is meant to be conveyed by this " THAT WHO " is the vaguest kind of indication, destitute of all relation or comparison. For, were anyone to ask, " What is the symbol comparable with or corresponding to this That ? " no answer to the question could be conceived. Now He Who transcends all relations is ALLĀH, the ONE REALITY. Thus, when certain Arabs once asked the Apostle of God, " To what may we relate Allāh ? " this reply was revealed, " *Say, He, Allāh is one ! His days are neither ended nor begun ; neither is He a father nor a son ; and none is like unto Him, no not one* " [2] ; the meaning of which verse is simply that He transcends relation. Again, when Pharaoh said to Moses : " *What, pray, is the Lord of the Universe ?* " as though demanding to know His essence, Moses, in his reply, merely indicated *His works*, because these were clearer to the mind of his interrogator ; and answered, " *The Lord of the heavens and the earth.* " [3] But Pharaoh said to his courtiers, " *Ha! marked ye that !* "

---

[1] See for this whole passage S. 6, 75–8.   [2] S. 112.

[3] For this passage see S. 26, 24–7, and for the whole thought compare pp. [54, 55].

as though objecting to Moses' evasion of his demand to be told Allāh's essential nature. Then Moses said, " *Your Lord, and your first fathers' Lord.*" Pharaoh then set him down as insane. He had demanded an analogue, for the description of the divine Essence, and Moses replied to him from His works. And so Pharaoh said, " *Your prophet who has been sent you is insane.*"

3. Fundamental Examples of Symbolism : especially from the Story of Moses in the Koran

Let us now return to the pattern we selected for illustrating the symbolic method. The science of the Interpretation of Visions determines for us the value of each kind of symbol ; for " Vision is a part of Prophecy ". It is clear, is it not, that the *sun*, when seen in a vision, must be interpreted by a Sovereign Monarch, because of their mutual resemblance and their share in a common spiritual idea, to wit, sovereignty over all, and the emanation or effusion of influence and light on to all. The antitype of the *moon* will be that Sovereign's Minister ; for it is through the moon that the sun sheds his light on the world in its own absence ; and even so, it is through his own Minister that the Sovereign [32] makes his influence felt by subjects who never beheld the royal person. Again, the dreamer who sees himself with a ring on his finger with which he seals the mouths of men and the secrets of women, is told that the sign means the early Call to Prayer in the month of Ramadan.[1] Again, for one who sees himself pouring olive oil into an olive-tree the interpretation is that the slave-girl he has wedded is his mother, unrecognized by him. But it is impossible to exhaust the different ways by which symbols of this description may be interpreted, and I cannot set myself the task of enumerating them. I can merely say that just as certain beings of the Spirit-World Supernal are symbolized by Sun, Moon, and Stars, others may be typified by different

---

[1] Because after the *idhān*, just before morning, food and sexual intercourse are fasted from till the next sunset.

symbols, when the point of connexion is some characteristic other than light.

For example, if among those beings of that Spirit-World there be something that is fixed and unchangeable ; great and never diminishing ; from which the waters of knowledge, the excellencies of revelations, issue into the heart, even as waters well out into a valley ; It would be symbolized by the *Mountain*.[1] Further, if the beings that are the recipients of those excellencies are of diverse grades, they would be symbolised by the *Valley*; and if those excellencies, on reaching the hearts of men, pass from heart to heart, these hearts are also symbolized by *Valleys*.[2] The head of the Valley will represent the hearts of Prophet, Saint, and Doctor, followed by those who come after them. So, then, if these valleys are lower than the first one, and are watered from it, then that first one will certainly be the " *Right* " *Valley*,[3] because of its signal rightness [4] and superiority. And finally will come the lowest valley which receives its water from the last and lowest level of that " Right " Valley, and is accordingly watered from " *the margin of the Right Valley* ",[5] not [33] from its deepest part and centre.

But if the spirit of a prophet is typified by a lighted *Lamp*, lit by means of Inspiration (" *We have inspired thee with* (a) *Spirit from Our power* "),[6] then the symbol of the source of that kindling is *Fire*. If some of those who derive knowledge from the prophets live by a merely traditional acceptance of what they are told, and others by a gift of insight, then the symbol for the former, who investigate nothing, is a *Fire-brand* or a *Torch* or a *Meteor* ; while the man of spiritual experience, who has therefore something in some sort common with the prophets, is accordingly symbolized by the *Warming*

---

[1] S. 28, 29, 46.

[2] S. 13, 18.

[3] S. 28, 30. See S. 19, 53, and 20, 82.

[4] Ghazzālī here plays on the word *ayman*, the root of which means *dexter* or *felix*.

[5] S. 28, 30.   [6] S. 42, 52.

of Fire, for a man is not warmed by hearing about fire but by being close to it.

If the first stage of prophets is their translation into the World of Holy Transcendence away from the disturbances of senses and imagination, that stage is symbolized by "*the Holy Valley*".[1]　And if that Holy Valley may not be trodden save after the doffing of the Two Worlds (that is, this world and the world beyond) and the soul's turning of her face towards the One Real (for this world and the world beyond are co-relatives and both are accidentia of the human light-substance, and can be doffed at one time and donned at another), then the symbol of the putting-off of these Two Worlds is the *doffing of his two sandals* by the pilgrim to Mekka,[2] what time he changes his worldly garments for the pilgrim's robe and faces towards the holy Kaaba.

Nay, but let us now translate ourselves to the Presence Dominical once more, and speak of its symbols. If that Presence hath something whereby the several divine sciences are engraven on the tablets of hearts susceptible to them, that something will be symbolized by the *Pen.*[3]　That within those hearts whereon these things are engraved will be typified by the *Tablet,*[4] *Book,*[5] and *Scroll.*[6]　[34] If there be, above the pen that writes, something which constrains it to service, its type will be the *Hand.*[7]　If the Presence which embraces Hand and Tablet, Pen and Book, is constituted according to a definite order, It will be typified by the *Form* or *Image.*[8] And if the human form has *its* definite order, after that likeness, then is it created "*in the Image, the Form, of the Merciful One*".　Now there is a difference between saying, " In the image of the *Merciful* One," and, " In the image of *Allāh.*"　For it was the Divine *Mercy* that[9] caused the image of the Divine Presence to be in that " Image ".　And then

[1] S. 20, 12, and 79, 16.　　[2] S. 20, 12.　　[3] S. 68.
[4] S. 85, 22, and 7, 44.　　[5] S. 2, 1.　　[6] S. 25, 3.
[7] S. 48, 36.　　[8] S. 82, 8 ; cf. 64, 3.
[9] See n. 1, p. 76.

Allāh, out of his grace and *mercy*, gave to Adam a summary
" image " or " form ", embracing every genus and species in
the whole world, insomuch that it was as if Adam were all
that was in the world, or were the summarized copy of the
world.   And Adam's form—this summarized " image "
was inscribed in the handwriting of Allāh, so that *Adam* is
the Divine handwriting, which is not the characters of letters
(for His Handwriting transcends both characters and letters,
even as his Word transcends sound and syllables, and His Pen
transcends Reed and Steel, and His Hand transcends flesh
and bone).   Now, but for this *mercy*, every son of Adam
would have been powerless to know his Sovereign-Lord ; for
" only he who knows himself knows his Lord ".   This, then,
being an effect of the divine mercy, it was " in the image
of the Merciful One ", not " in the image of Allāh ", that Adam
was created.   So, then, the Presence of the Godhead is not
the same as the Presence of The Merciful One, nor as the
Presence of The Kingship, nor as the Presence of the Sovereign-
Lordship ; for which reason He commanded us to invoke
the protection of all these Presences severaily.   " *Say, I
invoke the protection of the Lord of mankind, the King of
mankind, the Deity of mankind!* " [2]   If this idea did not
underlie the expression [35] " Allāh created man in the image
of the Merciful ", the words would be linguistically incorrect ;
they should then have run, " after His image." [3]   But the
words, according to Bokhari, run, " After the image of the
Merciful."

But as the distinction between the Presence of the Kingship
and the Presence of the Lordship call for a long exposition,
we must pass on, and be content with the foregoing specimen
of the symbolic method.   For indeed it is a shoreless sea.

But if you are conscious of a certain repulsion from this

---

[1] There must, I think, be some corruption in the text here.   I suggest

reading جَمَلَتْ for عَلَى.

[2] S. 114.   [3] And *so* they are quoted on p. [7].

symbolism, you may comfort yourself by the text, " *He sent down from heaven rain, and it flowed in the valleys, according to their capacity* " [1]; for the commentaries on this text tell us that the Water here is *knowledge*, and the Valleys are *the hearts of men.*

4. The Permanent Validity of the Outward and Visible Sign

Pray do not assume from this specimen of symbolism and its method that you have any licence from me to ignore the outward and visible form, or to believe that it has been annulled ; as though, for example, I had asserted that Moses had not really shoes on, or did not really hear himself addressed by the words, " *Put thy shoes from off thy feet.*" [2]   God forbid ! The annulment of the outward and visible sign is the tenet of the Spiritualists (*Bāṭiniyya*), who looked, utterly one-sidedly, at one world, the Unseen, and were grossly ignorant of the balance that exists between it and the Seen. This aspect they wholly failed to understand. Similarly, annulment of the inward and invisible meaning is the opinion of the Materialists (*Ḥashawiyya*). In other words, whoever abstracts and isolates the outward from the whole is a Materialist, and whoever abstracts the inward is a Spiritualist, while he who joins the two together is catholic, perfect. For this reason the Prophet said, " The Koran has an outward and an inward, an ending and a beginning " (a Tradition which is, however, possibly traceable to 'Alī, as its pedigree stops short at his name). I assert, on the contrary, that Moses understood from the command " *Put off thy shoes* " the Doffing of the Two Worlds, and obeyed the command *literally* by putting off his two sandals, and *spiritually* by putting off the Two Worlds. Here you just have this cross-relation between the two, [36] the crossing over from one to the other, from outward word to inward idea. The difference between the true and false positions may be thus illustrated.

[1] S. 13, 19.   [2] S. 20, 12.

One man hears the word of the Prophet, " The angels of Allāh enter not a house wherein is a dog or a picture," and yet keeps a dog in the house, because, he says, " The outward sense is not what was meant ; but the Prophet only meant, ' Turn the dog of Wrath out of the house of the Heart, because Wrath hinders the knowledge which comes from the Lights Angelical ; for anger is the demon of the heart.' "   While the other *first* carries out the command literally, and *then* says, " Dog is not dog because of his visible form, but because of the inner idea of dog—ferocity, ravinousness. If my house, which is the abode of my person, of my body, must be kept clear of doggishness in concrete form, how much more must the house of my heart, which is the abode of man's true and proper essence, be kept clear of doggishness in spiritual idea ! "   The man, in fact, who combines the two things, he is the perfect man ; which is what is meant when it is said, " The perfect man is the one who does not let the light of his knowledge quench the light of his reverence."   In the same way he is never seen permitting himself to ignore one single ordinance of religion, for all the perfection of his spiritual Insight.   Such a thing is grievous error ; an example of which is the evil which befel some mystics, who called it lawful to put-by literal prescriptions of the Shariat as you roll up and put-by a carpet ; insomuch that one of them perhaps went so far as to give up the ordinance of prayer, saying, forsooth, that he was always at prayer in his heart ! But this is different from the error of those fools of Antinomians (*Ibāḥiyya*) who trifle with sophisms, like the saying of one, " Allāh has no need of our works " ; or of another, " The heart is full of vices from which it cannot possibly be cleansed,'' [37] and did not even desire to eradicate anger and lust, because he believes he is [not] (?) commanded to eradicate them. These last, verily, are the follies of fools ; but, as for the first-named error, it reminds one of the stumble of a high-bred horse, the error of a mystic whom the devil has diverted from the way and " *drawn him with delusion as with cords* ".[1]

<hr>

[1] S. 7, 21.

To return to our discussion of "the Putting-off of the Shoes". The outward word wakens one to the inward signification, the Putting-off of the Two Worlds. The outward symbol is a real thing, and its application to the inward meaning is a real truth. Every real thing has its corresponding real truth. Those who have realized this are the souls who have attained the degree of the Transparent Glass (we shall see the meaning of this presently). For the Imagination, which supplies, so to speak, the clay from which the symbol is formed, is hard and gross ; it conceals the secret meanings ; it is interposed between you and the unseen lights. But once let it be clarified, and it becomes like transparent glass, and no longer keeps out the light, but on the contrary becomes a light-conductor, nay, that which keeps that light from being put out by gusts of wind. The story of the Transparent Glass, however, is coming ; meanwhile, remember that the gross lower world of the imagination became to the Prophets of God like a transparent " glass " shade and " a niche for lights "; a strainer, filtering clear the divine secrets; a stepping-stone to the World Supernal. Whereby we may know that the visible symbol is real : and behind it lies a mystery. The same holds good with the symbols of " the Mountain ", " the Fire ", and the rest.

5. Another example of this Two-sided and Equal Validity

When the Prophet said, " I saw Abdul-Rahmān enter Paradise crawling," you are not to suppose that he did not see him thus with his own eyes. No, awake he saw him, as a sleeper might see him in a dream, even though the person of Abdul-Rahmān b. 'Awf was at the time asleep in his house. [38] The only effect of sleep in this and similar visions is to suppress the authority of the senses over the soul, which is the inward light divine ; for the senses preoccupy the soul, drag it back to the Sense-world, and turn a man's face away from the world of the Invisible and of the Realm Supernal.

But, with the suppression of sense, some of the lights prophetical may become clarified and prevail, inasmuch as the senses are no longer dragging the soul back to their own world, nor occupying their whole attention. And so it sees in waking what others see in sleep. But, if it has attained absolute perfection, it is not limited to apprehending the visible form merely ; it passes direct from that to the inner idea, and it is disclosed to such an one that faith is drawing the soul of an Abdul-Raḥmān to the World Above (described by the word " Paradise "), while wealth and riches are drawing it down to this present life, the World Below. If the influences which draw it to the preoccupations of this world are more stubborn than those which draw it to the other world, the soul is wholly turned away from its journey to Paradise. But if the attraction of faith is stronger, the soul is merely occasioned difficulty, or retarded, in its course, and the symbol for this in the world of sense is *a crawl*. It is thus that mysteries are shown forth from behind the crystal transparencies of the imagination. Nor is this limited to the Prophet's judgment about Abdul-Raḥmān only, though it was only him he saw at that time. He passes judgment therein on every man whose spiritual vision is strong, whose faith is firm, but whose wealth has so much multiplied that it threatens to crowd out his faith, only failing to do so because the power of that faith more than counterbalances it. This example illustrates to you the way in which prophets used to see concrete objects, and have immediate vision of the spiritual ideas behind them. Most frequently the idea is presented to their direct inward vision *first*, and then looks down from thence on to [39] the imaginative spirit and receives the imprint of some concrete object, analogous to the idea. What is conferred by inspiration in waking vision needs explanation, just as what is conferred by inspiration in sleeping vision or dreams needs interpretation.[1]

---

[1] (*Note, by Ghazzāli.*) The proportion borne by dreams to the other characteristics of prophethood is as one to forty-six. That borne by

II. The Psychology of the Human Soul: its Five Faculties or Spirits

The gradations of human Spirits Luminous; in knowing which we may know the symbolism of the Light-Verse in the Koran.

The *first* of these is the *sensory spirit*. This is the recipient of the information brought in by the senses; for it is the root and origin of the animal spirit, and constitutes the differentia of the animal genus. It is found in the infant at the breast.

The *second* is the *imaginative spirit*.[1] This is the recorder of the information conveyed by the senses. It keeps that information filed and ready to hand, so as to present it to the intelligential spirit above it, when the information is called for. It is not found in the infant at the beginning of its evolution. This is why an infant wants to get hold of a thing when he sees it, while he forgets about it when it is out of his sight. No conflict of desire arises in his soul for something out of sight until he gets a little older, when he begins to cry for it and asks to have it, because its image is still with him, preserved in his imagination. This faculty is possessed by some, but not all animals. It is not found, for example, in the moth which perishes in the flame. [40] The moth makes for the flame, because of its desire for the sunlight, and, thinking that the flame is a window opening to the sunlight, it hurries on to the flame, and injures itself. Yet, if it flies on into the dark, back it comes again, time after time. Now had it the mnemonic spirit, which gives permanence to the sensation of pain that is conveyed by the tactile sense, it would not return to the flame after being hurt once by it. On the other hand, the dog that has received one whipping runs away whenever it sees the stick again.

waking vision has a greater ratio—as one to three, I believe, for it has been revealed to us that the prophetic characteristics fall definitely into three categories, and of these three one is waking vision.

[1] Aristotle's φαντασία.

Third, the *intelligential spirit*.[1] This apprehends ideas beyond the spheres of sense and imagination. It is the specifically human faculty. It is not found in the lower animals, nor yet in children. The objects of its apprehension are axioms of necessary and universal application, as we mentioned in the section in which the light of intelligence was given precedence over that of the eye.

Fourth, the *discursive spirit*.[2] This takes the data of pure reason and combines them, arranges them as premisses, and deduces from them informing knowledge. Then it takes, for example, two conclusions thus learned, combines them again, and learns a fresh conclusion ; and so goes on multiplying itself *ad infinitum*.

Fifth, the *transcendental prophetic spirit*. This is the property of prophets and some saints. By it the unseen tables and statutes of the Law are revealed from the other world, together with several of the sciences of the Realms Celestial and Terrestrial, and pre-eminently theology, the science of Deity, which the intelligential and discursive spirits cannot compass. It is this that is alluded to in the text, " *Thus did We inspire thee with a spirit from Our power. Thou didst not know what is the Book, nor what is Faith,* [41] *but we made that spirit a light wherewith we guide whom We will of our vassals. And thou, verily, dost guide into a straight way.*" [3] And here, a word to thee, thou recluse in thy rational world of the intelligence ! Why should it be impossible that beyond reason there should be a further plane, on which appear things which do not appear on the plane of the intelligence, just as it is possible for the intelligence itself to be a plane above the discriminating faculty and the senses ; and for revelations of wonders and marvels to be made to it that were beyond the reach of the senses and the discriminative faculty ? Beware of making the ultimate perfection stop at thyself ! Consider the intuitive faculty of poetry, if thou wilt have an example of everyday experience, taken

---

[1] Aristotle's νοῦς.   [2] Aristotle's διανοία.   [3] S. 42, 52.

from those special gifts which particularize some men. Behold how this gift, which is a sort of perceptive faculty, is the exclusive possession of some ; while it is so completely denied to others that they cannot even distinguish the scansion of a typical measure from that of its several variations. Mark how extraordinary is this intuitive faculty in some others, insomuch that they produce music and melodies, and all the various grief-, delight-, slumber-, weeping-, madness-, murder-, and swoon-producing modes ! Now these effects only occur strongly in one who has this original, intuitive sense. A person destitute of it hears the sounds just as much as the other, but the emotional effects are by him only very faintly experienced, and he exhibits surprise at those whom they send into raptures or swoons. And even were all the professors of music in the world to call a conference with a view of making him understand the meaning of this musical sense, they would be quite powerless to do so. Here, then, is an example taken from the gross phenomena which are easiest for you to understand. Apply this now to this peculiar prophetical sense. And strive earnestly to become one of those who experience mystically something [42] of the prophetic spirit ; for *saints* have a specially large portion thereof. If thou canst not compass this, then try, by the discipline of the syllogisms and analogies set forth or alluded to in a previous page, to be one of those who have knowledge of it scientifically. But if this, too, is beyond thy powers, then the least thou canst do is to become one of those who simply have faith in it (" *Allāh exalts those that have faith among you, and those who acquire knowledge, in their several ranks* ").[1] Scientific knowledge is above faith, and mystic experience is above knowledge. The province of mystic experience is feeling ; of knowledge, ratiocination ; and of faith, bare acceptance of the creed of one's fathers, together with an unsuspicious attitude towards the two superior classes.

You now know the five human spirits. So we proceed :

[1] S. 58, 11.

they are all of them *Lights*, for it is through their agency that every sort of existing thing is manifested, including objects of sense and imagination.   For though it is true that the lower animals also perceive these said objects, mankind possesses a different, more refined, and higher species of those two faculties, they having been created in man for a different, higher, and more noble end.   In the lower animals they were only created as an instrument for acquiring food, and for subjecting them to mankind.   But in mankind they were created to be a net to chase a noble quarry through all the present world ; to wit, the first-principles of the religious sciences.   For example, a man may, in perceiving with his visual sense a certain individual, apprehend, through his intelligence, a universal and absolute idea, as we saw in our example of Abdul-Raḥmān the son of 'Awf.

PART III.—THE APPLICATION TO THE LIGHT-VERSE AND THE VEILS TRADITION

I.   THE EXPOSITION OF THE SYMBOLISM OF THE LIGHT-VERSE

We now come to what the symbolism of this Verse actually signifies.   The full exposition of the parallelism between these five classes of Spirit, and the fivefold Niche, Glass, Lamp, Tree, and Oil, [43] could be indefinitely prolonged.   But we must be content with shortly indicating the method of this symbolism.

1. Consider *the sensory spirit*.   Its lights, you observe, come through several apertures, the eyes, ears, nostrils, etc. Now the aptest symbol for this, in our world of experience, is the *Niche* for a lamp in a wall.

2. Take next *the imaginative spirit*.   It has three peculiarities: first, that it is of the stuff that this gross lower world is made of, for its objects have definite and limited size, and shape, and dimension, and are definitely related to the subject in respect of distance.   Further, one of the properties of a gross substance whereof corporal attributes are

predicated is to be opaque to the light of pure intelligence, which transcends these categories of direction, quantity, and distance. But, secondly, if that substance is clarified, refined, disciplined, and controlled, it attains to a correspondence with and a similarity to the ideas of the intelligence, and becomes transparent to light from them. Thirdly, the imagination is at first very much needed, in order that intelligential knowledge may be controlled by it, so that that knowledge be not disturbed, unsettled, and dissipated, and so get out of hand. The images supplied by the imagination hold together the knowledge supplied by the intellect. Now, in the world of everyday experience the sole object in which you will find these three peculiarities, in relation to physical light, is *Glass*. For glass also is originally an opaque substance, but is clarified and refined until it becomes transparent to the light of a lamp, which indeed it transmits unaltered. Again, glass keeps the lamp from being put out by a draught or violent jerking. [44] By what, then, could possibly the imagination be more aptly symbolized ?

3. *The intelligential spirit*, which gives cognizance of the divine ideas. The point of the symbolism must be obvious to you. You know it already from our preceding explanation of the doctrine that the prophets are a " *light-giving lamp* ".

4. *The ratiocinative spirit.* Its peculiarity is to begin from one proposition, then to branch out into two, which two become four and so on, until by this process of logical division they become very numerous. It leads, finally, to conclusions which in their turn become germs producing like conclusions, these latter being also susceptible of continuation, each with each. The symbol which our world yields for this is a *Tree*. And when further we consider that the fruit of the discursive reason is material for this multiplying, establishing, and fixing of all knowledge, it will naturally not be typified by trees like quince, apple, pomegranate, nor, in brief, by any other tree whatever, except the *Olive*. For the quintessence of the fruit of the olive is its oil, which is the material which feeds

the lamps, and has this peculiarity, as against all other oils, that it increases radiance. Again, if people give the adjective " blessed " to specially fruitful trees, surely the tree the fruitfulness whereof is absolutely infinite should be named *Blessed* ! Finally, if the ramifications of those pure intellectual propositions do not admit of relation to direction and to distance, then may the antitypical tree well be said to be " *Neither from the East nor from the West* ".

5. *The transcendental prophetic spirit*, which is possessed by saints as well as prophets if it is absolutely luminous and clear. For the thought-spirit is divided [45] into that which needs be instructed, advised, and supplied from without, if the acquisition of knowledge is to be continuous ; while a portion of it is absolutely clear, as though it were self-luminous, and had no external source of supply. Applying these considerations, we see how justly this clear, strong natural faculty is described by the words, " *Whose Oil were well-nigh luminant, though Fire touched it not* " ; for there be Saints whose light shines so bright that it is " well-nigh " independent of that which Prophets supply, while there be Prophets whose light is " well-nigh " independent of that which Angels supply. Such is the symbolism, and aptly does it typify this class.

And inasmuch as the lights of the human spirit are graded rank on rank, then that of Sense comes first, the foundation and preparation for the Imagination (for the latter can only be conceived as superimposed after Sense) ; those of the Intelligence and Discursive Reason come thereafter. All which explains why the Glass is, as it were, the place for the Lamp's immanence ; and the Niche, for the Glass : that is to say, the Lamp is within the Glass, and the Glass within the Niche. Finally, the existence, as we have seen, of a graded succession of Lights explains the words of the text " *Light upon Light* ".

Epilogue: the Darkness-Verse

But this symbolism holds good only for the hearts of true believers, or of prophets and saints, but not for the hearts of misbelievers ; for the term " light " is expressive of right-guidance alone. But as for the man who is turned from the path of guidance, he is false, he is darkness ; nay, he is darker than darkness. For darkness is neutral; it leads one neither one way nor the other ; but the minds of misbelievers, and the whole of their perceptions, are perverse, and support each other mutually in the actual deluding of their owners. They are like a man " *in some fathomless sea, overwhelmed* [46] *by billow topped by billow topped by cloud ; darkness on darkness piled* ! " [1] Now that fathomless sea is the World, this world of mortal dangers, of evil chances, of blinding trouble. The first " billow " is the wave of lust, whereby souls acquire the bestial attributes,[2] and are occupied with sensual pleasures, and the satisfaction of worldly ambitions, so that " *they eat and luxuriate like cattle. Hell shall be their place of entertainment* ! " [3] Well does this wave represent darkness, therefore ; since love for the creature makes the soul both blind and deaf. The second " billow " is the wave of the ferocious attributes, which impel the soul to wrath, enmity, hatred, prejudice, envy, boastfulness, ostentation, pride. Well is this, too, the symbol of darkness, for wrath is the demon of man's intelligence ; and well also is it the uppermost billow, for anger is mostly stronger even than lust ; swelling wrath diverts the soul from lust and makes it oblivious of enjoyment ; lust cannot for a moment stand up against anger at its height. Finally, " the cloud " is rank beliefs, and lying heresies, and corrupt imaginings, which become so many veils veiling the misbeliever from the true faith, from knowledge of the Real, and from illumination by the sunlight of the Koran and human

---

[1] S. 24, 40.

[2] The following tripartite division of the soul, with its analogues, is Platonic (see *Republic*, bk. iv)

[3] S. 12, 47.

intelligence. For it is the property of a cloud to veil the shining of the sunlight. Now these things, being all of them darkness, are well called " *darkness on darkness piled* ", shutting the soul out from the knowledge of things near, [47] let alone things far away ; veiling the misbeliever, therefore, from the apprehension of the miraculousness of the Prophet, though he is so near to grasp, so manifest upon the least reflection. Truly it might be said of such an one that " *when a man putteth forth his hand, he can well-nigh see it not* ".[1] Finally, if all these Lights have, as we saw, their source and origin in the great Primary, the One Real, then every Confessor of the Unity may well believe that " *the man for whom Allāh doth not cause light, no light at all hath he* ".[1]

And now you must be content with thus much of the mysteries of this Verse.

II. THE EXPOSITION OF THE SYMBOLISM OF THE SEVENTY THOUSAND VEILS

What is the signification of the tradition, " *Allāh hath Seventy Thousand Veils of Light and Darkness : were He to withdraw their curtain, then would the splendours of His Aspect surely consume everyone who apprehended Him with his sight.*" (Some read " seven hundred veils "; others, " seventy thousand.")

I explain it thus. Allāh is in, by, and for himself glorious. A veil is necessarily related to those from whom the glorious object is veiled. Now these among men are of three kinds, according as their veils are pure darkness ; mixed darkness and light ; or pure light. The subdivisions of these three are very numerous. That much only is certain. I could no doubt make some far-fetched enumeration of these sub-divisions ; but I have no confidence in the results of such defining and enumerating, for none knows whether they were really intended or no. As for the fixing of the number at seven hundred, or at seventy thousand, this is a matter that only the prophetic power can compass. My own clear

---

[1] S. 24, 40.

impression, however, is that these numbers are not mentioned in the way of definite enumeration at all, for [48] numbers are not infrequently mentioned without any intention of limitation, but rather to denote some indefinitely great quantity :—God knows best ! That point, then, is beyond our competence, and all I can do now is to unfold to you these three main divisions and a few of the subdivisions.

1. Those veiled by Pure Darkness

The first division consists of those who are veiled by pure darkness. These are the atheists "*who believe not in Allāh, nor the Last Day*".[1] These are they "*who love this present life more than that which is to come*",[2] for they do not believe in that which is to come at all. They fall into subdivisions.

First, there are those who desire to discover a cause to account for the world, and make Nature that cause. But nature is an attribute which inheres in material substances, and is immanent in them, and is moreover a dark one, for it has no knowledge, nor perception, nor self-consciousness, nor consciousness, nor light perceived through the medium of physical sight.

Secondly, there are those whose preoccupation is Self, and who in no wise busy themselves about the quest for causality. Rather, they live the life of the beasts of the field. This veil is, as it were, their self-centred ego, and their lusts of darkness ; for there is no darkness so intense as slavery to self-impulse and self-love. "*Hast thou seen*," saith Allāh, "*the man who makes self-impulse his god ?*"[3] and the Prophet, "*Self-impulse is the hatefullest of the gods worshipped instead of Allāh.*"

This last division may further be subdivided. There is one class which has thought that this world's Chief End is the satisfaction of one's wants, lusts, and animal pleasures, whether connected with sex, or food, or drink, or raiment.

----

[1] S. 4, 37. [2] S. 14, 3. [3] S. 25, 43.

These, therefore, are the creatures of pleasure ; pleasure is their god, the goal of their ambition, and in winning her they believe that they have won felicity.   Deliberately and willingly do they place themselves at the level of the beasts of the field ; nay, at a viler level than the beasts.   Can darkness be conceived more intense than this ?   Such men are, indeed, veiled by darkness unadulterated.   Another class has thought that man's Chief End is conquest and domination—the taking of prisoners, and captives, and life.   [49] Such is the idea of the Arabs, certain of the Kurds, and withal very numerous fools.   Their veil is the dark veil of the ferocious attributes, because these dominate them, so that they deem the running down of their quarry the height of bliss.   These, then, are content to occupy the level of beasts of prey, ay, one more degraded still.   A third class has supposed that the Chief End is riches and prosperity, because wealth is the instrument for the satisfaction of every lust.   Their concern is therefore the heaping up and multiplication of riches—the multiplication of property, real estate, personal estate, thoroughbreds, flocks, herds, fields, and the rest.   Such men hoard their pelf underground—you may see them toiling their lives long, embarking on perils by land, perils by sea, up-dale, down-lea, piling up wealth, and yet grudging it to themselves—and how much more others !   These are they whom the Prophet had in view when he said, " *Poor wretch, the slave of money* ! *Poor wretch, the slave of gold* ! "   And, indeed, what darkness is intenser than that which blinds mankind to the fact that gold and silver are just two metals, unwanted for their own sakes, no better than gravel unless they are made a means to various ends, and spent upon things worth spending on ?   A fourth class has advanced a step higher than the total folly of these last, and has supposed that the supreme felicity is found in the extension of a man's personal reputation, the spread of his own renown, the increase of his own following and his influence over others.   You may see these admiring themselves in their own looking-glasses !

One of them, who may be suffering hunger and penury at home, will be spending his substance on clothes, and trying to look his smartest therein, [50] just in order to avoid contemptuous glances when he walks abroad !

Innumerable are the varieties of this species, and one and all are veiled from Allāh by pure darkness, and they themselves are darkness.   So there is no need to mention all the individual varieties, when once attention has been called to the species. One of these varieties which we should, however, mention is the sort that confesses with their tongues the Creed " There is no god but Allāh " but are probably urged thereto by fear alone, or the desire to beg from Mohammedans, or to curry favour with them, or to get financial assistance out of them, or, by a merely fanatical zeal, to support the opinions of their fathers.   For if the Creed fails to impel these to good works, by no means shall it secure their elevation from the dark sphere to light.   Rather are their patron-saints devils, who lead them from the light into the darkness.   But he whom the Creed so touches that his evil deeds displease him and his good deeds give him pleasure, has passed from pure darkness even though he be a great sinner still.

2. Those veiled by mixed Light and Darkness

The second division consists of those who are veiled by mixed light and darkness.   It consists of three main kinds : first, those whose darkness has its origin in the Senses ; secondly, in the Imagination ; thirdly, in false syllogisms of the Intelligence.

First, then, those veiled by the darkness *of the Senses*. These are persons who one and all have got beyond that self-absorption which was the characteristic of all the first division, as they deify something outside the self, and have some yearning for the knowledge of the Deity.   The first grade of these consists of the idol-worshippers, the last grade consists of the dualists ; between which extremes come other grades.

The first, the idolaters, are aware, in general, that they have a deity whom they must prefer to their dark selves, and believe [51] that their deity is mightier than everything else, and more to be prized than every prize. But the darkness of sense veils from them the knowledge that they must transcend the world of sense in this quest; so that they make for themselves from the more precious minerals, gold, silver, gems, etc., figures splendidly fashioned, and then take these images unto themselves as gods. Such men are veiled by the light of Majesty and Beauty from the attributes of Allāh and his light ; they have affixed these attributes to sense-perceived bodies ; which sense has blocked out the light of Allāh ; for the senses are darkness in relation to the World Spiritual, as we have already shown.

The second class, composed of the remotest Turkish tribes, who have no organized religious community and no definite religious code, believe that they have a deity, and that that deity is some particularly beautiful object ; so that when they see a human being of exceptional beauty, or similarly a tree, or a horse, etc., they worship it and call it their god. These are veiled by the light of Beauty mixed with the darkness of Sense. They have penetrated further than the idolaters into the Realm of Light in the discovery of Light, for they are worshippers of Beauty in the absolute, not in the individual ; and they do not limit it specially to one individual to the exclusion of others ; and then, again, the Beauty they worship is of Nature's hand, and not of their own.

The third class say, Our deity must be in His essence Light, glorious in His express image, majestic in Himself, terrible in His presence, intolerant of approach ; and yet He must be likewise perceptible. For the imperceptible is meaningless in the opinion of these. Then because they find Fire thus characterized, they worship it and take it unto themselves as lord. Such are veiled by the light of Dominion and of Glory, [52] which are, indeed, two of the Lights of Allāh.

The fourth class think that, since we have control over fire, kindling or quenching it at will, it cannot serve as divinity.

Only that which possessing the attributes of Dominion and Glory and has us under its absolute sway, and is withal very high and lifted up—only this avails for divinity. Astrology is the science that is celebrated among this folk, the attribution to each star of its special influence ; so that some worship Cynosura and others Jupiter, and others some other heavenly body, according to the many influences with which they believe the several stars are endued. These, then, are veiled by Light, the Light of the Sublime, the Luminous, the Potent ; which are also three of the Lights of Allāh.

The fifth class support the fourth in their fundamental idea, but they say that it does not befit their Lord to be describable as small or great among light-giving substances, but He must be the greatest of them ; and so they worship the Sun, which, they say, is the Greatest of All. Such are veiled by the Light of Greatness, in addition to the former lights ; but are still blent with the darkness of the Senses.

The sixth class advance higher still and say, The sun has no monopoly of light ; bodies other than the sun have each one its light. So, as the deity must have no partner in lightfulness, they worship Absolute Light, which embraces all lights, and think that It is the Lord of the Universe, and that all good things are attributable to it. Then, since they perceive the existence of evils in the world, and will by no means allow them to be attributed to their deity, He being wholly void of evil, they conceive of a struggle between Him and the Darkness, [53] and these two are called by them, as I suppose, Yazdān and Ahrimăn ; which is the sect of the Dualists.

This must suffice for the exemplification of this division, the classes whereof are more numerous than those we have mentioned.

Second, those veiled by some light, mixed with the darkness of *the Imagination*. These have got beyond the senses, for they assert the existence of something behind the objects of sense, but are unable to get beyond the imagination, and so have worshipped a Being who actually sits on a throne. The meanest grade of these is called the Corporealists ; then all the various Karrāmites, into whose writings and opinions we cannot go here, for to multiply words thereon were bootless. But the highest in degree are those who denied to Allāh corporality and all its accidentia, except one—*direction*, and that *direction upwards* ; for (say they) that which is not referable to any direction, and cannot be characterized as either within or without the world, does not exist at all, since it cannot be imagined by the imagination.[1] They failed to perceive that the very first degree of the intelligibilia takes us clean beyond all reference whatsoever to direction and dimension.

Third, those who are veiled by Light divine, mixed with the darkness of false syllogisms of *the Intelligence*, and who worship a deity that " Heareth, Seeth, and hath Knowledge, Power, Will, Life ", and transcends all direction, including direction upwards ; but whose conception of these attributes is relative to their own ; so that some of them may even have declared outright that His " speech " is with sounds and letters like ours ; while others advanced a step higher, it may be, and said, " Nay, but it is like our thought-speech, both soundless and letterless." Thus, when they were challenged to show that " hearing, sight, life ", etc., are *real* in Allāh they fell back on what was essentially anthropomorphism, though they repudiated it[2] formally ; for they utterly failed to apprehend what [54] the attribution of these ideas to Allāh really signifies. Thus they say, in regard to His will, that it is contingent, like ours; that it is a demanding and a purposing, like ours. All of which opinions

---

[1] See Averroes, opusc. cit., p. 61, Cairo ed., p. 51.

[2] It seems inevitable to read اِنْكَرُوه. The feminine pronoun could only refer to حَقِيقَة, which makes nonsense. To refer it to a supplied *maṣdar* does not seem to be in our author's manner.

are well kr^ ҳn, and we need not go into further details with
regard to them. These, then, are veiled by several of the
divine Lights, mixed with the darkness of false syllogisms of
the intelligence. All such are various classes of the second
division, which consists of those veiled by mixed light and
darkness.

3. Those veiled by Pure Light

The third division are those veiled with pure Light,
and they also fall into several classes. I cannot enumerate
all, but only refer to three.

The *first* of these have searched out and understood the true
meaning of the divine attributes, and have grasped that
when the divine attributes are named Speech, Will, Power,
Knowledge, and the rest, it is not according to our human
mode of nomenclature. And this has led them to avoid
denoting Him by these attributes altogether, and to denote
Him simply by a reference to His creation, as Moses did in
his answer to Pharaoh, when the latter asked, " *And what,
pray, is the Lord of the Universe ?* " and he replied, " ' *The
Lord, Whose Holiness transcends even the ideas of these
attributes,' He, the Mover and Orderer of the Heavens.*" [1]

The *second* mount higher than these, inasmuch as they
perceived that the Heavens are a plurality, and that the mover
of every several Heaven is another being, called an Angel,
and that these angels form a plurality, and that their relation
to the other Lights Divine is as the relation of the stars to [2]
all other visible lights.[3] Then they perceived that these
Heavens are enveloped by another Sphere, by whose motion
all the rest revolve once in twenty-four hours, and that finally
The LORD is He Who communicates motion to this outermost
Sphere, which encloses all the rest, on the ground (say they)
that plurality must be denied of Him.

---

[1] See S. 26, 23 ff. [2] Reading اِلى for فِى. [3] Cf. S. 41, 11.

The *third* mount higher than these also, [55] and say that this direct communication of motion to the celestial bodies must be an act of service to the Lord of the Universe, an act of worship and obedience to His command, and rendered by one of His creatures, an Angel, who stands to the pure Light Divine in the relation of the Moon to the other visible lights ; and they asserted that the LORD is the Obeyed-One of this Angelic Movent, and that the Almighty must be considered the universal Movent indirectly and by way of command only (*amr*),[1] but not directly by way of act. The explication of which " command " and what it really is contains much that is obscure, and too difficult for most minds, besides being beyond the scope of this book.

These, then, are grades all of which are veiled by Lights without admixture of Darkness.

4. The Goal of the Quest

But those who ATTAIN make a fourth grade, to Whom, in turn, it has been made clear that this Obeyed-One, if identified with Allāh, would have been given attributes negative of His pure Unity and perfection, on account of a mystery which it is not in the scope of this book to reveal ; and that the relation of this Obeyed-One to THE REAL EXISTENCE is as the relation of the Sun to Essential Light, or of the live coal to the Elemental Fire ; and so " turned their faces " [2] from him who moves the heavens and him who issued the command (*amara*) for their moving, and Attained unto an Existent who transcends ALL that is comprehensible by human Sight or human Insight ; for they found IT transcendent of and separate from every characterization that in the foregoing we have made.

And these last are also divided. For one class the whole content of the perceptible is consumed away—consumed, obliterated, and annihilated ; yet the soul itself remains

<hr>

[1] See S. 7, 53.   [2] See M., pp. [30, 31].

contemplating the absolute Beauty and Holiness, and contemplating herself in her beauty, which is conferred on her by this Attainment unto the Presence Divine. [56] In them, then, the seen things, but not the seeing soul, are obliterated.

And they are passed by others, among whom are the Few of the Few; whom "the splendours of the Countenance sublime consume",[1] and the majesty of the Divine Glory obliterate; so that they are themselves blotted out, annihilated. For self-contemplation there is no more found a place, because with the self they have no longer anything to do. Nothing remaineth any more save the One, the Real; and the import of His word, "*All perisheth save His Countenance,*"[2] becomes the experience of the soul. To this we have made reference in the first chapter, where we set forth in what sense they named this state "Identity", and how they conceived the same.

Such is the ultimate degree of those who Attain. Some of these souls had not, in their upward Progress and Ascent, to climb step by step the stages we have described; neither did their ascension cost them any length of time; but with their first flight they attained to the knowledge of the Holiness and the confession that His sovereignty transcends everything that it must be confessed to transcend. They were overcome at the very first by the knowledge which overcame the rest at the very last. The onset of God's epiphany came upon them with one rush, so that all that is apprehensible by the sight of Sense or by the insight of Intelligence was by "the splendours of His Countenance utterly consumed". It may be that that first was the way of Abraham, the Friend of Allāh, while the latter was the way of Mohammed, the Beloved of Allāh. Allāh alone knoweth the mysteries of their Progress and of their Stations on the Way of Light.

Such is our account of the classes of the veiled by the Veils; and it were not strange if, after all these Stations were fully classified and the veils of the Pilgrims Mystical were

---

[1] See the Tradition on p. [2].   [2] S. 28, 88.

fully studied, the number of classes were found to amount to Seventy Thousand. Yet, if you look carefully, you shall find that of them all not one falls outside the divisions which we have set forth. For, as we have shown, they must be veiled by their own human attributes ; *or* by the senses, imagination, discursive intelligence ; *or* by pure light.

This is what has occurred to me by way of answer [57] to your interrogations, though these came to me at a time when my thought was divided, and my mind preoccupied, and my attention given to other matters than this. May not my suggestion be, then, that you ask forgiveness for me for anything wherein my pen has erred, or my foot has slipped? For 'tis a hazardous thing to plunge into the fathomless sea of the divine mysteries ; and hard, hard it is to essay the discovery of the Lights Supernal that are beyond the Veil.

THE END.